A Journey through Many Worlds

An Epic Voyage through Worlds of Adventure
including the Amazon, Angola, Iraq and Afghanistan

Johan Dempers

Copyright © 2017 by Johan Dempers

All rights reserved. This book or any portion thereof may not be reproduced or used in any manner whatsoever without the express written permission of the publisher except for the use of brief quotations in a book review or scholarly journal.

First Printing: 2017

Wellington, South Africa

www.expeditionearth.info

Introduction by Eeben Barlow

We seldom hear or read of men who still fit the mould of 'adventurer'. I am proud to know one such man and to have shared time working with him.

Johan Dempers is a man who follows his heart and his passion - one of a seldom-encountered breed of man in the politically correct and backbone-lacking world we live in...

Comparing him to a modern day Indiana Jones is grossly unfair. Johan is real and Indi is nothing but a storybook character who would be hard pressed to match Johan's adventures. No comparison can ever be made between the two.

As a man, he has played a part in many great adventures and travels across the globe – from the desperate and bloody battlefields of Angola to desolation and dangerous fields of Iraq and Afghanistan.

Despite severe injuries, he has never abandoned his love and passion for adventure and the Amazon trip is a perfect example of a man with drive and gumption – a man who is not put off by the unknown. He will face it as the man I know he is.

In the pursuit of his dreams, Johan has trekked over 15 000 km across South America. He has faced heat, bitter cold and snow, excitement, sorrow and danger. He was once captured by wild Indians in the Amazon and was fortunate to escape becoming their lunch. Not many men can lay claim to that.

Johan does not do this for himself, nor does he keep his voyages of discovery hidden...He shares these incredible quests with readers, scholars, teachers and researchers alike, giving us all a chance to share the footprints he and his small team of likeminded adventurers have made and relive what they have experienced and seen.

He is a well-known professional photographer that has captured many incredible images through his lens. These are not mere photographs; they are pieces of art and great beauty that capture the soul and essence of a man at one with nature. They are real, and not posed. They open doors to worlds hitherto unknown to most of us.

I can think of no greater honour than being asked to write a few words on a remarkable man.

Johan Dempers is one of a dying breed, and a man I am proud to know. He is indeed one of the last of the real adventurers.

I wish him well as he continues to journey through many worlds.

Eeben Barlow

Pretoria, 2017

Eeben Barlow is a former South African Defence Force Lieutenant-Colonel. He saw active service in conventional, clandestine and covert units of the SADF. He was also the founder of the Private Military Company (PMC) Executive Outcomes in 1989 and trained SADF Special Forces in Covert Operations.

Table of Contents

(The Latest) Foreword	1

Book I: Off to the Amazon

Acknowledgments	3
Authors Preface	5
Chapter 1 : An Advertisement in the newspaper	7
Chapter 2: En route to Peru, land of the Inca	15
Chapter 3: Across the Andes — Mountain World of mystery	25
Chapter 4: Machu Picchu—City of Secrets	39
Chapter 5: Walking on water—Journey to the lake in the clouds	44
Chapter 6: Nazca—Sketchbook of the Ancients	51
Chapter 7: Entering the River World of the Amazon jungle	56
Chapter 8: Up the Ucayali—Headwater of the Amazon	64
Chapter 9: Meeting Marco Polo and friends — Good Men Doing Bad Things	74
Chapter 10: The Long Road to Sawawo	85
Chapter 11: Down the "River of Dreadful Turns"	97
Chapter 12:Captured by Campa Indians— the Chief has Spoken	129
Chapter 13:Rescued and recovering under the Southern Cross	147

Table of Contents

Chapter 14: In a leaking Indian canoe down
the most winding river on Earth 151

Chapter 15: On the Amazon—Heading for Manaus 185

Chapter 16: The end? 187

Book II: Return to Riverland

Chapter 1 : Back to Reality and off Again! 190

Chapter 2: Time-warp 2005 —Waking up in a
different world 197

Chapter 3: Against all Odds—Mission Afghanistan
and back to Jordan and Iraq 209

Chapter 4: Some Thoughts 213

Chapter 5: 15 Years later—A new Adventure unfolds 215

(The Latest) Foreword

Let's start with a short intro... The book you are holding in your hand was not a 'planned' project or endeavour... the original story line started a decade and a half ago in a world much different from our current world in many ways.

But many other things will always be with us. Things like Life and Death... and some other good and bad in between. This book is a story I want to share. It's my story and about my thoughts and encounters in my world. A little bit of history and some other interesting facts are also added. Please accept it as it is—written by me and mainly for me to complete one of my journeys which I started many years ago.

After our original 6 month Amazon Expedition which started in 2002, a lot of things changed in the world and in my personal life. And yes some definitely because of the 6 month absence too. Leaving your world and people for a prolonged time can for sure sometimes have a drastic impact on your life.

If I were put back in the same situation today... would I do it again? Hell, YES! I would without any doubt. In retrospect it was the best decision I ever made.

In the second part of the book you can read about my more recent travels.

Johan Dempers, 25 July 2017

"The real question is not whether life exists after death. The real question is whether you are alive before death.

—Osho Rajneesh

Book I: Off to the Amazon

Acknowledgments

It would have been impossible to write this book without the help, contributions, and effort of so many people in my life. To everybody involved—whether it was with suggestions, proof reading, supplying material, or a word of motivation—I am forever grateful.

Joe, my companion and oldest friend—I salute you!

Arthur, at "Base Camp" in South Africa, for his immense efforts behind the scenes who made everything possible. We can never repay you. The Indians of Acre, Brazil, for not eating us. Senhor Renato of the Brazilian Civil Police in Thaumathurgo, for rescuing us from the Indians (and for giving us bread)

Federal Agents De Almeida, Ogata, Machete, and the rest of the Brazilian Federal Police at Cruzeiro do Sul, for the free flight to Cruzeiro and their professional handling of the situation. Daniella at Banco do Brazil, Cruzeiro do Sul, the best (and most beautiful) ambassador of Brazil, for her help and smile.

Jens Herf for donating money to buy another canoe at Cruzeiro do Sul. Captain Bob Webb of, for relaying that money halfway around the globe in 30 minutes. The Unknown Boatsman at Eirunepe, for stealing the above-mentioned canoe. Daniela from Durban for translations.

Christian of AGFA in Cape Town for sponsoring my 35mm films. SONY for supplying Joe's miniDV cassettes. Bruce Tretheway of Leatherman for sponsoring the best tools ever. It really made a difference. AVNIC ELECTRONICS for lending us a GARMIN GPS 76.

Gary Bergh of ENERGIZER for the batteries. Antoinette at South African Airways for her friendly help Esther at Butterfly World Paarl, for identification of the insects photographed & Don for his horribly honest comments.

A Journey through Many Worlds

Arthur, Johan, Albert, Neels, Niel, Bob, Clemens, Gavin and many others for making me realize what true friendship and support is.

You made my dream a reality.

JJD 2003

+ + + + + +

Journey through **Many Worlds** started off as **Journey through Two Worlds** and took nearly 15 years to complete and in only 10 days we are departing on our new Journey.

Salute to everyone who is making our new Adventure possible.
Canon South Africa is our main sponsor and they are supplying us with the best equipment to use, including a Canon 1DX Mk2 as well as a Canon 5D Mk4 with a great selection of lenses and equipment to the value of R 250 000.
Bruce of **Leatherman South Africa** gave us their great tools again as well as other support. Heinrich Welthagen of **Radio2Radio** is looking after our communication. Please have a look and support them, as well as our other sponsors that can be viewed at www.expeditionamazon.info
Eeben Barlow, I learned a lot from you - thank you. Also for the introduction. It was more than I could ever have asked for.
Bryan 'Snakehips' Donaldson, a Selous Scouts veteran who stood next to me early one morning, long ago, facing an RPG7 rocket launcher and many soldiers. Thanks, my dear friend, for all you have done in the life & death reality of Iraq.
Thank you Muldene - my Superwoman, Joe - my oldest friend and Hennie - my long-time friend, I am honored to have you by my side. Thank you Herman Smit for sponsoring the first printing of this book and Zhane Nel for your amazing personality and help! Erik Marais, thanks for all you have done. I am very priveledged to have such support.

JJD August 2017

Authors Preface

This book was intended to be the story of my journey. The act of putting it to paper resulted in an even greater journey of discovery.

"You're crazy! Why did you do it?" I heard this question hundreds of times, and I do not know the real answer. Because I had to. Or maybe because I haven't done it before.

I believe many people dream about doing a crazy thing like this. Luckily there are only a few who are actually crazy enough to do it. Whatever the reason—we did it, survived it, and now can share it with you. The idea of writing this book was born late one night, somewhere on the idyllic, white, mosquito infested beaches of the Jurua River in Brazilian Amazon.

What follows is a story about two South Africans, Joe Brooks and Johan Dempers, who decided to embark on a journey into the unknown. A journey that took us 15,000 kilometers across the South American continent—from ancient ruins of long lost civilizations, over the snow capped Andes mountains and into the rain forests of the Amazon basin—through some of the remotest and wildest regions on the face of our planet. It is an extraordinary story about two ordinary people. Our capture by Indians deep in the jungle of Brazil made international news, but that was only a small fraction of an incredible adventure. It was both a physical as well as a spiritual journey across a continent shrouded in mystery and legend. This book will take you, the reader, along with Joe and myself on an adventure of a lifetime—a journey through two worlds. Let us continue, the plane is taking off soon!

Johan Dempers 2003

This, my first book, is dedicated to my Mother and Father.

I will always remember you.

"Death must be so beautiful. To lie in the soft brown earth, with the grasses waving above one's head, and listen to silence. To have no yesterday, and no to-morrow. To forget time, to forgive life, to be at peace."

Mark Twain

Chapter 1
An Advertisement in the Newspaper

*"Grab a chance, and you won't be sorry for
a might have been."*

—Arthur Ransome

An advertisement in a South African newspaper, sometime in the early 1980's: "Members wanted for Amazon Expedition."

As I read these words, I visualize myself, machete in hand, hacking open a pathway through the dense South American jungle. Young explorer, about to make significant discoveries. Sure, I am only in my very early teens, but I know I can do it! But life is not always as we would like it to be....

"Mom! Look Here!" I read the advertisement to my ever patient mother, who seems to as always only respond by rolling her eyes heavenward—apparently looking for help.

"Yes, Johan..." "Doesn't it sound great, Mom?" I look hopefully for her reaction, oblivious to the fact that it has already been given. "My son, as long as you stay under this roof, you can forget about it. Now please go and do your school homework so that you can one day do whatever you choose!

Yuk. School was always—for me anyway—a terrible waste of time, and I submitted to it with great difficulty and under duress. The best part of school so far was playing with clay in first grade and making my first successful gunpowder last year. It's amazing what you can learn by reading.

Blissfully ignoring my mother's reaction, I go to my room;

A Journey through Many Worlds

taking the big green Reader's Digest Atlas of the World with me. I paged through to South America. Imagine exploring the ancient Inca ruins of Peru, the Amazon rainforests and its lost civilizations, treasures and, traveling on the planets biggest river. Imagine following the tracks of famous explorers like Colonel Percy Fawcett on a magical continent ... Imagine.

+ + + + + +

Then, sometime in 2002...

"Sir, would you please switch that instrument OFF!" The voice of the air stewardess on the SAA Drakensberg from Johannesburg to Sao Paolo is firm, although her smile appears convincingly genuine.

I wonder if it is a result of the 9/11 terrorist attacks that I cannot use the GPS on the Boeing. According to the instrument in my hand, we are flying at 889 km/h at an altitude of 11 259 meters above the Atlantic Ocean, about 2066 kilometers from Sao Paolo, Brazil. It seems like yesterday that I saw Joe Brook's advertisement:

"Fellow photographer wanted for an expedition to South America and the Amazon."

It appeared on the 28th of February 2002 in a local newspaper. With a flash of nostalgia, I thought of the conversation with my mother all those years ago—unfulfilled dreams from my childhood. Imagine...

Driven by pure curiosity, I answered the advertisement the same day, following the instructions to call a Joe Brooks. He was not available, but his girlfriend, Sally, said Joe would call me back.

Later the same day, Joe did call me back, and he told me that he last visited South America 39 years ago and that he now, at the age of 64, wanted to go back on an expedition down the Jurua River.

To be honest, I had never even heard of this river before, but it was, Joe assured me, one of the Amazon River's major tributaries. Joe added that he had received a few responses

An Advertisement in the Newspaper

to his advertisement, and if I was really interested, I must come and see him. At the time I ran a one man business—aerial photography—from my rented house in Paarl, Western Cape, about 60 kilometers from Cape Town.

February is a busy time of the year for aerial photography in South Africa, and the adventurous sounding advertisement was quickly forgotten. I remember telling a friend about it, and that I would at the very least meet with this Joe. Any person who at his age wants to tackle such an adventure must be worth at least meeting, I thought. But then I promptly forgot to contact Joe again, and life seemed to move on. I could in any event never afford it, I figured, but hell, it is nice to dream.

Then, at the beginning of March, Joe contacted me again, to find out if I was still interested. There and then I made an appointment to go and see him in the neighboring town of Somerset West. Joe and Sally live on a small holding nestling against the Helderberg Mountains and received me with great hospitality.

Sitting outside in the garden, Joe spread a map of South America over a table and showed me where the Jurua River ran its crinkly path from Peru to the Amazon. The thin Englishman explained with a great calmness that he had decided upon this river because it was the most remote one he could find. The first stage, he explained was to locate the origin of the river in Peru and then partly by canoe, and then later by log raft, travel the full length of the river—several thousand kilometers.

The canoe, he said, he would buy somewhere, and the log raft, why that was even easier. He would build it when he needed it. From the River's mouth, he would then travel using local conventional means to Manaus in Brazil, and from there back to São Paulo. The purpose of the expedition, he explained, was to make a documentary, in both video and still film.

To get a detailed view of the area, proved a little more difficult, and without thinking of the implications, I volunteered to get a map of the region from Microsoft

9

A Journey through Many Worlds

Encarta's Atlas. Joe felt that the expedition could take up to six months, and although by this stage I was abuzz with interest, in my heart I knew that this was not very practical. Six months off work? However, I returned home that evening with the knowledge that I wanted to go on this expedition. Joe could not give me even a reasonable guess as to what the costs were going to be.

I knew that my rent, cellular telephone contract, and other minor bills alone, added up over that period and were going to be a small fortune by themselves—and then of course for six months I would not be able to generate any income at all.

The possibility that the expedition could even generate any revenue from the video or still photography was also an open question. The bottom line was this: 'guaranteed expenditure' versus 'guaranteed no income'. After a long well thought through analysis of the situation, I decided to do what any good businessman would not do: I picked up the telephone and called Joe: "Joe, I'm in!"

"Excellent, Johan. We must get together as soon as possible. I want to leave in June at the latest" Shortly after that, Joe came to visit me in Paarl, and we began looking for information about our intended route on the Internet. To my great surprise, we could find almost nothing of value about our planned route!

Nowhere could I find any detailed maps of the Jurua, and Microsoft's Encarta Atlas remained our best bet: I printed out the map on 22 sheets of A4 paper and had each laminated.

Hours of planning followed. Over dozens of cups of coffee, detailed lists started to emerge of what we would need for this expedition. I called a friend in Johannesburg who had experience in public relations, to tell him of our plans.

He drew up a begging letter, disguised as a "Proposal for Sponsorship" and we sent it out to prospective sponsors, with only three months to go before our departure.

As the expected "We regret to inform you" answers rolled in, there was a surprise: a few days later AGFA in Cape Town called me and asked how much films we needed: 150 slide

An Advertisement in the Newspaper

(transparency) films would be sufficient, thank you!

Christian at AGFA then announced that our request was approved and that we could collect the films at the end of May.

A satellite telephone company expressed interest in the project, but when they heard we would have their equipment for at least six months, and possibly longer, they got cold feet. We thought it no great loss: a telephone is not really going to be of much use in the middle of the jungle if we hit serious trouble, but it is still the thought that counts. Sony in Johannesburg provided a batch of miniDV cassettes to Joe at a reduced price, and Bruce Trethewey from Tremac, the Leatherman agency, agreed to give us two Leatherman multi-tools at a giveaway price.

I was particularly happy about this acquisition as a Leatherman can do the job of a whole bag of tools. Gary Bergh from Energizer supplied us with a multitude of batteries. A GPS (Global Positioning System) is one of the most used instruments for the modern traveler.

Twenty four satellites, equipped with atomic clocks, are positioned 17,000 kilometers above the earth, and through signals sent out by these satellites, a GPS can determine your exact position, speed, and altitude above sea level. Avnic Electronics, the agents of GARMIN GPS, let us know from Johannesburg that they would provide us with the GPS 76, a maritime instrument, at no cost.

The GPS 76 is about as big as an old style cellular telephone, watertight and is driven by a power source of only 3 volts. It was wonderful to see the pieces of the plan start to fall into place. Friends and acquaintances from all over the place who heard of the expedition offered help, and many wanted to come along!

Joe was however adamant that he was not going to take more than one other person. "I've heard too many stories of things that went wrong because of too many people," Joe said.

There was one person that I really wanted to bring with

A Journey through Many Worlds

me, Neels van der Westhuizen, an old friend and long time adventurer. An ex-policeman, and former member of the South African elite Special Task Force, Neels had just returned from a hiking expedition to Nepal and was keen for even more adventure.

However, I had to respect Joe's decision and leave Neels behind. Bob Saayman, yet another one of my slightly strange collection of friends, called me one evening and invited me over for dinner. At his house, over a few beers, I told him of the plans. "I guess you know that you're fucking crazy, Johan?" was his reaction, but then, just as quickly, he continued: "I have something you must take along, just don't fuck it up." Bob is a straight-to-the-point person with a preference for high tech gadgets.

And he did not disappoint: from a drawer he took a Russian infrared night vision scope. "Go and watch the bloody Jaguars with it."

I knew Bob well enough to know that he wanted to take part in this adventure as well. He is an Africa expert who has extensive experience traveling across Africa in his converted Toyota Hilux pickup (according to Bob, this is the only sensible mode of transport on the planet). In 1992, he and I planned a photographic expedition to the south eastern battlefields of Angola, but unfortunately, another civil war that erupted in that country put paid to our plans.

Since then we had drawn up many exciting, but beer soaked plans and had never brought any of them to fruition. Then a new drama popped up: my passport had decided to expire, so I had to apply for a new one, a lengthy and frustrating process in South Africa.

The fingerprint forms vanished, and halfway through the whole affair, I had to provide new ones. I got the new passport just in time. And now: another potential hitch: according to information we had received, visitors to Peru were only allowed to bring five films per person into the country.

Something to do with espionage, we were told, although we never quite confirmed this. In any event, this was

12

An Advertisement in the Newspaper

obviously a problem as I intended to carry 150 films with me and Joe would have at least 40 mini DV cassettes with him. Not wishing to be arrested in Peru at the very start as spies for who knows what, we launched inquiries as to what to do with the Peruvian embassy in Pretoria.

After much too-ing and fro-ing, they decided that we should register as journalists, and this would grant us immunity from that peculiar law. With less than a week to go, we couriered our passports to Pretoria, had the necessary visas and permissions inserted, and then re-couriered back down to Cape Town.

The Department of Internal Affairs in Lima, Peru, was also informed of our visit, and we were instructed to collect our press ID cards in Lima once we had landed. My Karrimor Jaguar 8 backpack had already done its fair share of duty, seeing action in Namibia, Mozambique, and Angola. The trouble was, it looked like it too, but I have always had a special relationship with this bag—it would just not be fair to leave it behind on this adventure.

About three weeks before I had seen Joe's advertisement, I had fortuitously purchased a three man tent. This size was perfect for our purposes. Other equipment I bought included a self-inflating mattress which weighed less than one kilogram, a Petzl Tikka lamp with a battery lifetime of 150 hours, a decent Kershaw hunting knife, a thermometer/compass combination, a poncho and an X-Country Goretex jacket.

With our departure date looming, Joe made the sensible suggestion that we go away for a weekend to hone our camping skills. On the farm Doornrivier near Worcester, we tested our equipment. It was a cold, but otherwise pleasant few days, during which we also got to know each other a bit better. Around a large campfire, watched over by the Southern Cross, we sat and discussed possibilities of what may lie ahead.

I was particularly impressed with Joe's video equipment—a Canon XM1 digital video camera. He rigged a solar panel

A Journey through Many Worlds

to recharge the batteries—a very practical system that saves a hell of a lot of space and weight. Medical supplies, we decided, were of great importance. Dr. Patrick Fieuw from Paarl helped us greatly in this regard with advice and suggestions for a list of supplies which we should take with us. I had only allowed one kilogram for medical supplies, and he had expressed his concern that we had only budgeted for such a small amount. It was unfortunately not possible to take everything that we wanted to. Space and weight were of the greatest concern. For malaria, we decided on Mefliam as a generic alternative to Larium, along with four Malaria Test kits.

Louis Nel, another friend with extensive practical experience as an operational medic in the military also provided us with valuable tips and information. The last few days in South Africa flew by.

A journalist at the Cape Argus, Murray Williams, came to hear of the expedition and did an interview with Joe and me: the resulting article titled, "Slowly down the Amazon," appeared on Saturday 15 June, two days after our departure. Joe came to sleep at my house on the evening of the 12th of June. We packed the kit, and after I had made final arrangements with my girlfriend with regards to my aerial photography business, it was already 04h00 on the morning of 13 June. There was just enough time to jump into the shower before we had to leave for the airport.

At Cape Town International Airport, I said my goodbyes to my friends Bernice and Ilse. My hand baggage consisted of a watertight Pelican case with the much vaunted 150 rolls of films, and my camera bag. The nice lady at the X-Ray counter quickly lost her gentle countenance when I asked that my 150 films be subjected to a hand search. After a few anxious moments, and many "final calls for passengers Brooks and Dempers" we were allowed on our way and taken with a bus to the waiting flight 304 to Johannesburg. Two hours after arrival at Johannesburg International Airport, all 150 films were hand searched once again, and several minutes later Joe, and I sat down in our seats in row 50 of the Boeing 747-200 to São Paulo. The adventure had officially started.

Chapter 2
En Route to Peru, Land of the Inca

"Once a journey is designed, equipped, and put in process a new factor enters and takes over. It has personality, temperament, individuality, uniqueness. A journey is a person in itself; no two are alike."

—John Steinbeck (1902–1968)

After a flight lasting 9 hours and 30 minutes, it felt somehow good to be standing on solid earth again. São Paulo, which lies on the eastern coast of Brazil, has a population of nearly 10 million which easily makes it the biggest city in South America. A curtain of smoke hangs permanently over the city, pollution driven by its many industries. I am the first to go through customs, and after I indicate that I have nothing to declare, a suspicious customs agent decides otherwise and motions me to one side. In a long, narrow office with many tables which await the contents of passengers' bags, officials begin to open my belongings. A lady in uniform doing the searching lifts my sleeping bag and peeks at what lies beneath—virtual survivalist's requisition list. I hold my breath.

"It's OK; you can go... NEXT!" As I repack my bags, I wonder what the requirements for the job of a customs official in Brazil are. In the meanwhile, Joe has waltzed through customs, and now, more than half an hour later, I find him in an agitated state in the arrivals hall. "You can relax now Joe; I was only abducted by customs. " We will spend the evening at the Mercure Hotel in the suburb of Guarulhos and will leave the next morning for the capital of Peru, Lima. After a good dinner, we retire to our rooms

A Journey through Many Worlds

on the 11th floor for a well-earned rest. At half past seven the next morning, Joe knocks on my door. After breakfast, we set out to reconnoiter the area around the hotel. There seems to be an inordinately large number of dentists and attorneys in the suburb, and I can't help but wonder if they are somehow related to each other.

Later in the day, I take a free taxi to the nearby International Shopping Mall and am astounded at the range of goods on sale there. Our Varig flight only leaves at 19h00, and after a five-hour flight, we land in Lima at 22h00, Peruvian time. Lima's arrivals hall is horrifically busy, and hundreds of faces with characteristic Indian features are there to greet and stare at us.

All of them seem to be punting taxis to us, and Joe, after engaging in what seems like the haggling contest of the century, takes me to a US $5 bus. Our accommodation will be a guest house, Rodas 1, situated in the Avenida Petit Thouars. Also on board this bus is a group of three Americans, one of whom is an obviously nervous elderly woman, who just cannot shut up for one minute.

I suspect her nervousness is related to the traffic rules of Lima, or rather the lack thereof. A few meters away from each stop street, the bus driver blasts his hooter twice and then accelerates straight through the stop. It seems as if this is the local manner with which stop streets are dealt with.

The city seems to be as busy as the arrivals hall, and a holiday like atmosphere prevails, even though it is now nearly midnight. We race past a Pizza Hut, a McDonald's and a Kentucky Fried Chicken, all with their gaudy neon lights a-flashing, and I wonder which one Atahualpa would have chosen tonight.

At Rodas, we are welcomed by our friendly host, Roxanna. She is about 26 and comes from a small town in the Amazon. After dragging our baggage up the stairs to the guesthouse, we book in and Roxanna shows us our room. It is a plain affair, with two single beds adorned with covers which have seen better days. It also transpires that the other guests have already used up all the hot water and after an invigorating

En Route to Peru, Land of the Inca

cold shower I retire to my bed.

At 07h00 the next morning, we are up and start the day with a breakfast consisting of an omelet, three bread rolls with butter and jam, and some very excellent coffee. Now it is once again time to reconnoiter the surrounding area. Rodas is near the sea, in the Miraflores suburb of Lima.

It is a peaceful and tree rich area, with lovely old buildings and modern shops. Criminal activity in the suburb is apparently less than elsewhere and in central Lima, where tourists are warned not to enter while wearing jewelry and carrying cameras or other valuable items.

After nearly being knocked down several times by vehicles seemingly driven by the Devil himself (I will take a while to adjust to the fact that here they drive on the right-hand side of the road, unlike in South Africa), we reach a travel agent where we will attempt to find out more about our intended route and schedule.

"You cannot travel on your own in the Huancavelica/ Ayacucho area. It is dangerous!", the friendly travel agent lady tells us, after first offering us the by now ubiquitous coffee. Precisely why it is so dangerous, she appears not to know, but Joe suspects it has something to do with the activities of the Shining Path. The Shining Path, also called "Sendero Luminoso," is a communist militant group dating back to the 1960's. Its aim is the overthrow of the Peruvian government in favor of a communist state.

Although the organization has been hampered by the arrest of its charismatic leader, Abimael Guzman and his successor, Oscar Durand, their continued campaign has allegedly seen the death of around 30,000 people to date.

Illegal drug trafficking allegedly contributes to the continued financing of this group. Only a few months ago, shortly before the visit of President George W. Bush, a car bomb exploded outside the US embassy in Lima. A total of 9 people were killed and 30 injured.

As an alternative to certain death, the travel agent lady offers us one of her nicely advertised but unaffordable tourist

A Journey through Many Worlds

packages intended for adventurous overpaid Americans. With the last gulp of coffee, and a friendly 'no thanks,' we leave in search of something to eat.

We stop at a street café in one of the poorer areas of the city, and order the advertised 'menu.' The starter consists of an interesting soup. Floating in the watery, transparent liquid is a lone chicken foot and certain other pieces of an internal organ which look like they come from parts of a chicken which we usually never see. At the very least, they could have cut the chicken foot's nails, really!

The main course is considerably more appetizing. It consists of a piece of beef (at least, this is what I decide upon while considering the alternatives), rice, salad, and onions. An excellent chili sauce rounds off the dish. At 5 Soles, including a fruit juice, this interesting meal is real value for money for any poor and hungry tourist anyway.

For most of the year, a cold misty fog, called the Garua, hangs over Lima and a part of the west coast of Peru. It creates a depressing atmosphere, and today is no exception. Later that evening, we watch some TV.

There is unrest in Arequipa, apparently as a result of the sale of two state controlled electricity supply stations to a Belgian company. While Roxanna explains this to us in her broken English, we see on the screen how the police shoot at a crowd of people while a vehicle burns furiously in the background.

Joe and I look at each other—we had planned to visit Arequipa after stopping at Lake Titicaca. We look at the two other clients in the guesthouse lounge. One is John, a tall, hilariously funny Scotsman with a penchant for Bacardi rum. He entertains us with a monolog detailing his colorful adventures in South East Asia.

Then there is Bernie, an American of few words (yes... there are some of them!). His big, wild, pop-out eyes create the impression that he has just lost a chess match with the grim reaper. He is, however, a computer programmer and thinker, who spends a significant amount of his time writing

En Route to Peru, Land of the Inca

letters to big companies complaining about their products and then enjoying the 24 tins of condensed milk or whatever they send him to keep his mouth shut.

No-one asks him what he is doing in Lima. Bernie, however, is very interested in our planned expedition and makes us promise to meet him on the 24th—the day of the Inca's Sun Festival—at Cuzco. He leaves for Cuzco tomorrow morning already, he tells us.

Having absorbed far too much Bacardi, I stagger off to bed with a book lent to me by John. It is titled "Dead Famous."

The next two days are spent preparing ourselves for the first part of our adventure, namely the route through Peru. First stop is the Ministerio Relaciones Exteriores in downtown Lima to get our press IDs.

It turns out to be a complicated process which takes several hours. Outside the building, dating from colonial times, stand dozens of men with crossed arms, black suits, and dark glasses. Luxury 4x4 SUV's with tinted windows and strange looking antennae are parked in the street. There is also a large and visible police and military presence, and in stark contrast, a group of long haired journalists and photographers lounge nearby. I have a sense of déjà vu, somehow I have seen almost the identical scene in Africa in years gone by; it was a story of lying politicians, an imminent coup, political unrest...

We pack our rucksacks with the equipment we will need for the Peru part of our route. The rest of the stuff—like Joe's steel trunk and my travel bags—will wait for us in storage in our guest house, Rodas until we hopefully return in a month's time.

My bags, without the camera equipment, weigh 21 kilograms. At the Cruz del Sol agency, we buy bus tickets to our next destination, Huancayo. At the ticket price of 35 Soles each, it seems cheap to me to break out of Lima's perpetual mist and to experience the Andes Mountains.

Joe goes to sleep early on the evening of the 17th, while I chat to two new guests. Juliette and her friend are two

A Journey through Many Worlds

attractive Dutch blondes who have just finished a five-week tour of Peru. While we play cards and drink red wine, the conversation races back and forth, covering topics as different as Apartheid and Tarantulas.

The morning of 18 June dawns and Joe wakes me at 06h00. I have never been a morning person, and getting up is, without a doubt, the most difficult part of the day for me. Even though today is vital, it is still with mixed feelings that I hobble into the shower. Bonus: this morning the water is hot, and it cheers me up. By 07h00 we are in a taxi on our way to the bus terminal.

While our baggage is loaded into a luxury Volvo bus, the strains of Alphaville's 'Big in Japan' can be heard on a radio in the background. Hours later, a white snow wonderland unfolds before our eyes as the bus motors its way ever higher into the Andes.

Lunch is served by a cute girl dressed in what seems to be an air stewardess`s outfit. The meal is unremarkable—a pale piece of cooked meat, rice, two peas and a piece of carrot. Eight and a half hours after we leave Lima, we arrive in the city of exhaust fumes and half-built buildings—Huancayo. The half built building effect is generated by the fact that steel girders stick out of the roof of most of the buildings.

It transpires there is a good reason for this—state tax is only payable upon completed buildings, and so most people are always still building on their houses, even if in name only. While we are looking for a place to stay, Joe and I stop at a street café which appears to be very clean and neat.

The food, which vaguely reminds me of chicken ala king, turns out to be very good and a steal at only 3 Soles. We book into the "Hotel Comfort" and pay 30 Soles for a double room.

The next day we visit the sandstone formations of Torre, led by our newly acquired 'tour guide'—a young boy who understands not a word we say but eagerly shows us the way. It looks like tourists are a rarity here. Later in the day, we take a taxi to the pre-Inca ruin of Wariwilka, near Huari. There is also a museum which contains a bizarre looking

En Route to Peru, Land of the Inca

human skull in the shape of a cone.

We have spent the whole day walking, and we are now thoroughly exhausted—it will obviously take a bit of time to get used to the thin air of the Andes. At one of Huancayo's many markets, I buy an Alpaca jersey for 20 Soles.

The next day, Joe and I take the train to Huancavelica. It is an amazing 6-hour ride with stunningly beautiful postcard nature scenes along the way. I cannot describe the excitement as the train sometimes sways dangerously on its narrow tracks through this wonderland.

Before we reach our destination, the sky turns black as the day comes to an end. Then a bright beam of light appears from the top of the train. Somebody with a spotlight is apparently helping the train driver out...

I will in all honesty not remember the Hotel Camacho at Huancavelica for its cleanliness or friendly service. Two beds, each with six blankets, stand on the bare cement floor of our hotel room, and a filthy communal bathroom with cold water only and no toilet seat is situated up the passage. But then again, at 7 Soles each, we are in no position to complain. After a cold night's rest at 12,400 feet above sea level, we drink a cup of coffee, book out of the hotel and walk to the central square, Plaza de Armas.

Viceroy Francisco de Toledo founded Huancavelica in 1572 as a mining town and the famous Santa Barbara mercury mine is located nearby. The town is very clean with friendly people. On the Plaza, we are surrounded by a group of school children, and are subjected to demands for our autographs! I have no idea what went on in their minds, but they ran around enthusiastically comparing their prized autographs, and only left us alone after half an hour of this madness.

The bus only leaves at 06h00 for Santa Ines. It is a cold, wild ride, and through the misted bus windows I catch glimpses of snow lying deep next to the road. By now I have noticed that there is an image of Mother Mary in the front of every bus. I seem to see a worried look on her little face as the driver races fearlessly along the road, defying the fearsome

A Journey through Many Worlds

ravines with their blood-curdling drops into the abyss below. She must work overtime protecting this lot.

Feeling a little shaken, but relieved to be out of the bus, we arrive some two hours later at a dark Santa Ines. The icy thin air burns my lungs.

Our quarters for the night consist of a flat roofed 'house' which has no windows and whose main construction element appears to be blue plastic sheeting. Inside, a few paraffin lanterns burn half heartedly, and a middle aged man offers us a cup of weak coffee. It still tastes good. According to my thermometer, it is minus 7 degrees Celsius and still busy dropping.

In spite of the six blankets that press down heavily on me, I still find it difficult to sleep. I get incredible headaches, and it is very difficult to breathe. Altitude sickness can strike any traveler who moves quickly to a height of 8,000 feet or more above sea level.

In severe cases, it can lead to water on the lungs or swelling of the brain, both of which can be fatal. Here at 15,800 feet above sea level—higher than any place in the Alps—we are already deep in the danger zone, and I am starting to get gravely concerned about the strange half gargling, half snoring, type noises emanating from Joe's pile of blankets.

"Are you ok, Joe?" "No! I'm concentrating on trying to breathe," he replies in a weak voice. Neither of us actually sleep this night, and by half past six, we are up, still suffering from crushing headaches. Outside the 'house,' I see a little stream of solid frozen water.

Just after 07h00, a massively overloaded Volkswagen bus rumbles into the town. It's our transport. With Joe in the last available seat, and I jammed into whatever space I can find between the other passengers and the gear lever, we set off. I endure considerable discomfort in this position until we reach a police checkpoint at the Rumichaka Bridge, where we disembark. While we wait next to the road, one of our fellow passengers entertains us with his guitar and song. Here I see for the first time a real Condor high above us,

En Route to Peru, Land of the Inca

sweeping through the cloudless blue sky.

This enormous vulture-like bird has a wingspan of up to 3.25 meters and features strongly in the cultures and tales of this mountain world. Only at 15h00 does a bus arrive to take us further on our journey Two hours, forty minutes and 5 Soles later, we reach Ayacucho, a Quechua word which means "corner of the dead."

Ayacucho and environs have been witness to almost constant violence from the pre-Inca times right through to today—and is possibly most notorious as the birth place of the Shining Path. Peru declared its independence in 1821, and in 1824, the last Spanish force was defeated in the area Ayacucho by a combined Peruvian and Columbian army. This final battle settled the reality of Peruvian independence from Spain.

Today, the city has more than 100,000 inhabitants. After we have booked into the comfortable room 19 of the Hostel Crillonesa, we go for a meal of lomo saltado—a tasty dish of beef on rice. The rooms are clean, neat and they even have their own bathrooms with lukewarm water!

Ayacucho is, however, a dirty city with small streets. Apart from our lodgings, there seems to be little else to recommend it for. Sunday, the 23rd of June, greets us. Tomorrow it is the traditional Sun festival of Inti Raymi. We are however still quite a way from Cuzco, and it seems sad to think that we will now miss this colorful Inca festival.

We set off through Ayacucho, in the direction of Cuzco, on a dusty dirt road, carrying our backpacks which seem to be getting heavier. A friendly local, his vehicle packed with potatoes, takes pity on us and gives us a lift to his farm—only about 2.5 hours from the city.

As we take our leave from the potato farmer, we wish him all the best and a huge harvest. He asks us for a memento, and I give him the last of my South African money—a Five Rand coin. The countryside changes color in the final light of the sun as we set up our tent in the bush alongside the road.

A Journey through Many Worlds

We prepare ourselves for another cold night, all too aware that we do not have six blankets apiece this time. Just after sunset, the temperature is already minus five degrees. Our dinner consists of a tin of sardines, one avocado, and two rolls.

Then we creep into our sleeping bags and steel ourselves against the bitter Andean cold.

Chapter 3
Across the Andes,
Mountain World of Mystery

"The fairest thing we can experience is the mysterious. It is the fundamental emotion which stands at the cradle of true art and true science. He who knows it not and can no longer wonder, no longer feel amazement, is as good as dead, a snuffed-out candle."

—Albert Einstein

It is the 24th of June and a special day on the Inca calendar. Inti Raymi, the sun festival, lures tens of thousands of visitors to Cuzco. As we promised Bernie, the big eyed yank, we would be there. The reality is however that when we woke up on the morning of the 24th, frozen solid after a night in the tent, we were still very far from Cuzco.

As we packed the last of our goods into our backpacks, a silver 4x4 pickup appeared on the road. Dropping my rucksack, I ran towards the road, waving my arms.

In the dust, I catch a glimpse of red brake lights, and I run closer. My attempted Spanish is greeted in English by a big blond girl: "Do you guys need a lift?"

"Por favor . . . er . . . Yes please!" I reply. "We're on our way to Cuzco." 'We are not going that way, but if you are not in too much of a hurry, you can come with us to the Inti Raymi Sun Festival celebrations near Vilcashuaman," comes the reply. We end up on the back of the double cab on top of a few tires. It is a very bumpy ride on the poor dirt road,

A Journey through Many Worlds

and after about two hours of this exquisite torture, we find ourselves at the ruins near Vilcashuaman.

Hanke, the blond Dutch girl in the pickup, works for one of the European Union's projects in the area. She explains that the valley was, until recently, a stronghold and training area for the Shining Path and that the local population suffered terribly as a result. According to Hanke, there is also a small runway nearby which was used for cocaine smuggling.

We take our seats amongst the audience which has gathered opposite to the place where the ceremony is going to be held. I accept a cup of chicha from the moon faced Indian woman, who pours the concoction out of a green jerry can.

Chicha is a local alcoholic drink made from corn. The fermentation agent in the original recipe was the saliva of old women who first had to chew the corn before it was left to ferment a bit . . . It is a hot day, and in the valley, well, there was nothing else to drink, and I must admit that the second mug tasted better than the first. I will not inquire as to how original this chicha recipe is....

The locals appear to be very interested in our camera equipment, and when the festival began around 13h00, some of them were clearly far more interested in watching us than their celebrations.

The scene which played itself out was probably identical to that of a hundred or more years ago. The Winter Solstice of Inti Raymi was the single most important event on the Inca calendar and originally lasted several days.

It was preceded by several days of fasting, during which no fires were lit either. Everyone waited barefoot for the sunrise in the east, and as soon as the sun was visible, they sat greeting the sun with outstretched arms. After several other rituals, the Sun, as the father of the first Inca, was appeased by the ritual sacrifice of a llama. While the animal is still alive, its heart, still beating, is cut out and held triumphantly aloft by the Inca. Somewhere I have heard that the original festival was done with human sacrifices, but no one seems to mention that today...

Across the Andes

While the llama's blood-curdling screams die down, I turn round and have a look at the rest of the audience behind us. Some just sit and stare emotionless at the events, and others are laughing.

I wonder if they have a little more 'sun blood' in their veins than the others. . . Joe is disgusted with the poor llama's fate, and I can just catch a string of mumbled curses and swear words emanating from him. Then hundreds of Indians begin dancing and playing their flutes, and the ceremony comes to an end in a mass of swirling bodies.

It is now late in the afternoon. Joe and I begin to walk back to where the vehicle is parked, and Hanke indicates to us that we must get into the back of the mayor's red double cab Nissan Patrol.

By the time we get to that vehicle, five other locals have already boarded, and it is with a spot of difficulty that we get space to 'sit.' The resulting trip to Vilcashuaman is the most uncomfortable to date.

Apart from the fact that there is no space to sit, it seems as if the mayor is getting in some practice for his Formula One Grand Prix aspirations, tearing over the dirt road, oblivious to the spider like attempts of his passengers to remain onboard.

It is dark by the time we reach Vilcashuaman. Hanke shows us where the best residence in the town is. Like most places in the Andes, everything is centered around the Plaza de Armas, or square, located in the center of the town. To win the prize of 'Best Hotel in Vilcashuaman,' the owner had to ensure that his guests were provided with hot water.

The only other hotel had to be happy with runner up status. In return for her help and friendliness, we invite Hanke to have dinner with us that evening. We first, however, want to book into the hotel and put our bags down. A young man of about 20, books us in, making sure we sign our names in a register and taking 14 Soles for the night. He proudly tells us that there is hot water in this hotel, in a manner which makes it seem like he is talking about the latest technology

27

A Journey through Many Worlds

on earth.

We indicate that after dinner, we would be honored to partake in this technological miracle.

While we sit in the only eating house in the area, Hanke tells us that she has only seen five tourists in the past two months in the town. The meal costs 3.5 Soles and consists of soup, Saltado Caserul, and a weak mint tea.

We thank Hanke again and walk back to the hotel through the plaza. It was an exhausting day, and I can feel the effect of the sun god upon my face. Somewhere I will have to buy sun block.

Back at the hotel, I cannot wait to have my hot water shower. Disrobed, I turn on the tap. There is no hot water. In fact, there is no water at all.

Highly pissed off, I call the young receptionist and parade him in front of Joe with his better-translating skills in an attempt to solve the problem.

After a long conversation, discussion and question time which would give the Spanish Inquisition a run for its money, we finally extract from him the truth that the water in Vilcashuaman is cut off between 20h00 and 06h00 every day.

Mr. Hotel Manager does not know why this is, and he appears to be genuinely taken aback that this seems inconvenient to us. I gain the impression that he thinks that all towns in the world have their water supply cut off at night.

Next morning, the water is indeed back on, but it is cold. I give it half an hour, thinking that it might take a little while to warm up. This hope is in vain, and we then do the Peruvian thing—shower in cold water.

I am learning that it does not help to complain to the locals too much: you will just get old and die dirty, having achieved nothing. Near our hotel, there is an Inca 'pyramid', or Usno platform—the only one of its type in Peru.

28

Across the Andes

The construction is in the form of a terrace going upwards where it ends in a flat top about 15 x 12 meters wide. A 'throne' made out of solid stone, seating two, is located on this flat top, offering a splendid view of the valley. My neck tingles as I sit in the chair, wondering what transpired here all those centuries ago.

There are so many questions and secrets locked away in this country, most of them which will probably never be answered.

Alongside the plaza, there is a stone which was apparently used to sacrifice children. It is time once again to push on. This time we get a taxi bus out of the town to where the Cuzco road starts, about three hours and 7 Soles later.

We find another police control point here, and after Joe explains to them where we are going, they tell him that it is impossible to get a lift to Cuzco from there.

Many hours later, an old truck stops and allows us to climb on its back. It seems as if there are only two speeds in Peru: extremely fast or extremely slow. The truck trundles off at a sedate 25 km/h, and the 60 kilometers to Orcos seems to take forever. The road is in a terrible condition, small with kinks around the seemingly impossible hairpin bends and vast valleys below. At one stage a truck going the other way nearly knocks our truck into the valley.

Although the ride took ages, it was certainly not without more than enough tension. We disembark outside Orcos and walk into the town with our luggage on our backs.

First stop is a garage where Joe buys fuel for his portable stove. A group of kids follows us as we walk into the town. It must look bizarre, and images of the Pied Piper of Hamelin play in my mind.

Small, dusty and unknown, Orcos is centered around another Plaza de Armas. There is, however, no hotel here, but we find a police station.

This is one of the most interesting police stations I have ever seen in my life, and believe me when I tell you I have

29

A Journey through Many Worlds

seen a few. Mother Mary, clutching a baby Jesus, looks down through a cracked glass frame on the dirty window ledge at Fonzi, the off-white dog. Fonzi has a peculiar face—maybe there was a Golden Retriever in his ancestry somewhere in the remote past, but for the rest of it, he looks like a Peruvian pavement special.

Whatever the case, a trained and alert police dog he is not, and even our entrance into the office does not disturb his slumber on the three-seater imitation leather couch where he lies stretched out in all his canine glory. It is apparent that he has a long history of dog fights behind him and a closer inspection reveals that it seems unlikely that he won any of them.

On the table next to the couch is a Yaesu radio, and alongside that, a desk with an Olivetti typewriter. Manning the typewriter is Christian, a thin man who comprises a third of the town's police force.

He and his colleagues are very friendly and after inspecting our passports, become even friendlier. Christian insists that we sleep in the barracks, while he and his colleagues sleep in the charge office.

The police 'barracks' consists of two particularly filthy rooms without electricity, built on top of the police station. Joe sums it up when he turns to me and says under his breath: "This is a bloody rats' nest!"

It is a kind offer of free lodging which we accept with mixed feelings. Christian brings the further good tidings that there is a bus to the next town at 7h00 the next morning. He asks us a lot about South Africa, and it is apparent there are not very many visitors to this town.

Another revelation comes when he asks me if I know how some of the settings on the police radio works. They are using a Yaesu radio and a while later I figured out how the "squelch" setting can produce a more quiet work environment for the officers and more restful nights for Fonzi.

After we have made coffee for the police force of Orcos, we set off for the only eating house in the town. While there, we

30

Across the Andes

ask to use the bathroom—a small outbuilding which leads from the kitchen.

In the kitchen there is a sight to behold: we are so fascinated that we stop in mid walk to take in the stunning effect of a few women dressed in black, with hats, standing round a huge black pot. Orange flames lick up around the pot from the open fire upon which it sits. Joe and I instantly name the place 'Macbeth's.'

The food which is ultimately generated from this Shakespearean scene looks like it has already been through someone else's digestive system.

After two attempts to ingest it, Joe decides that it is better to go to sleep hungry. My food, something resembling chicken curry on rice, tastes considerably better than its appearance indicates, and I enjoy as much of it as I can while I try hard to shut the image of the kitchen out of my mind.

Back at our free quarters, I stoically ignore the all pervasive odor and throw my ground sheet over the bed in an attempt to ward off bed bugs and who knows what other residents of the mattress. I drift into an uneasy state of rest.

Needless to say, we are up bright and early at 6h00, and well in time for the 07h00 bus. As we stand expectantly, we start chatting to one of the locals, who casually informs us that there is no 07h00 bus, but only one at 10h00!

We stand there depressed, but there is little we can do. To our great surprise, the bus arrives at 08h45, and with our last 10 Soles, we start the journey to Andahuaylas.

Just over five hours later, we reach the small town. Another piece of good fortune strikes us: Joe finds a working ATM, draws some money and we book into the Hostel Americano.

I can no longer wait to get to Cuzco: this endless run around is finishing me.

Before we leave the next day, Joe decides to finally test his stove by cooking twelve eggs on the roof of the hotel. Also, we buy fruit and some rolls for supplies, and at 13h00 we leave for Abancay. The bus is, as usual completely overloaded, and

A Journey through Many Worlds

the passage between the seats is jam packed full of standing, crouching, sitting, belching and farting passengers.

Now and then we hear a muffled noise from the back of the bus: "Baaa"—an animal of some sort is also on board.

I look around and after a while spot a woman sitting peacefully looking out of the window while a small goat of some sort sits in a bag alongside her.

I look up in boredom and see an Epson Stylus printer in the roof rack, sandwiched between the luggage. The contrast cannot be more vivid—here sits a goat in a bag, and there is a high tech computer printer. Funny world, this. Land of contrast.

Suddenly the passengers all begin talking loudly, and some start laughing, pointing out of the window. I peer hard, and then someone screams as the bus driver slams on anchors.

Then I see it: through one of the windows on the other side of the vehicle, I see a sheep's leg dangling down. I realize that the poor animal is actually part of the baggage tied to the roof of the bus.

During one of the wild turns the bus made, the sheep must have managed to loosen itself from its fellow suitcase and other bag prisoners. It then started cunningly, but unintentionally, to escape by sliding down the side of the bus.

Unfortunately for this modern Houdini, an alert passenger had spotted it. Once the sheep had been refastened to the roof, we set off on our way again. For the first time, I notice the interesting shadow the bus casts with the surfing sheep on top.

+ + + + + +

Almost 60 kilometers from Abancay, we can see the small town nestling deep in the valley. The view is astronomical.

Abancay was established in 1540, and its name comes from a local flower called the 'amankay.' The town is located

Across the Andes

close to 2.4 kilometers 7800 feet) high in the Peruvian Andes mountains.

'Hostal Samy' is not located in the best place in town— directly opposite the noisy bus company HQ. Our first-floor room is sparsely furnished, and there are no pictures on the walls. But its true beauty is that it has real hot water! An inspection of the bathroom reveals another bonus: the toilet has a seat! Now that is a luxury indeed in this mountainous world.

We decided to celebrate this discovery and find a place to buy rolls, berry jam and rum. One can just see that one is nearer a tourist center because even though the town is not so large, there is all manner of restaurants, pubs, and shops selling tourist type items.

At a cheap shop in one of the side streets, I buy a wide brimmed hat for 6 Soles. After my introduction to the Peruvian sun during Inti Raymi, this was high on my list of priorities.

Back at the Hostel, I enjoy one of the best showers I have had in a long time, and then spend the rest of evening listening to Joe's entertaining stories from his colorful past. Amongst other things, he spent ten years in Japan as an English teacher, and as a photographer and traveler, he has visited more than 50 different countries.

At about 23h00 we drift off to sleep, in spite of the noise from the busy street below. We get up nice and early and buy bus tickets at the 'Espresso Wari' across the road for a mere 15 Soles each. According to the ticket, the bus leaves at 8h00, but the man behind the counter assures us that it actually only leaves at half past eight. At a quarter to ten, we finally leave.

The road to Cuzco is tarred, and the journey is comfortable. After 13h00 we arrive at the city's bus depot, which looks a bit like an airport. The road was long, and I buy an 'Inca Cola' to quench my thirst. This is a yellowish soft drink which does not taste too bad and is the local opposition to Coca Cola. There are many tourists here, and while we take

A Journey through Many Worlds

a taxi to the Plaza de Armas, we spot lots more parading in the streets. Cuzco is situated in the Huatanay River valley, at an altitude of about 11,200 feet above sea level and has a population of over a quarter of a million.

Once at the plaza, we saddle up our rucksacks and start searching the town for accommodation. The city has a lively buzz of its own, and after what seems like an almost never ending march up a paved side street, we reach the Hostel 'Apu Wasi.' The dried out wooden gate leading to the inside is opened by a round faced man of distinct Asiatic ancestry with very prominent front teeth.

At 35 Soles, the accommodation is cheap by Cuzco's standards, and this price includes a flask of 'coca tea.' To make this, you take dried coca leaves, boil them in water and mix with sugar. It is very enjoyable and is reputed to be a stimulant.

The Incas apparently also used it to provide extra energy and good fortune. There are many legends and tales involving Coca and the Inca empire. It has also been chewed by natives for thousands of years and used as medicine, to help against hunger and even as an aphrodisiac. Coca is of course well known worldwide for its psychoactive alkaloid, cocaine. The Coca plant is a shrub that grows wild in South America up to more than 4 meters high! Talking about "Coca." It rings a bell, doesn't it? It's like the first part of "Coca Cola."

In 1863 a Corsican chemist named Angelo Mariani produced a very popular tonic drink and medicine using coca leaves and Bordeaux wine, and he called it "Vin Mariani."

This drink was patented, and it was a huge success especially in America and Europe. It was so popular that even among royalty such as Queen Victoria and King George. The great American inventor and businessman, Thomas Edison (Inventor of the light bulb, the motion picture camera) also endorsed the drink and claimed it helped him to stay awake longer.

Many other world famous people including writers like Sir Arthur Conan Doyle and Jules Verne also enjoyed this

Across the Andes

drink and it even ended up in the Vatican where Pope Leo VIII awarded a Vatican gold medal to it and also appeared on a poster endorsing it!!

This fantastic and popular drink apparently inspired a former Confederate army officer with the name John Pemberton from Atlanta in Georgia, USA to produce a similar drink. Coca Cola originally contained cocaine, but it was phased out many years ago and replaced with caffeine.

While Joe sorts out our room, I take my camera and go for a walk down the steep Pumacurco Street in the direction of a small square, the Plaza Nazarenas. Once there, I turn right and follow the small alley until I get to the big plain, the Plaza de Armas. It is something like the main square in many Hispanic American cities.

Some type of festival is under way, and dozens upon dozens of children in brightly colored costumes come dancing past in groups, all around the square, to the accompaniment of flutes and drums. Tourists and locals alike gather to watch the spectacle.

The camera flashes and drums mix in a weird almost hypnotic manner to produce a surreal effect. My attempts to find out what exactly the festival is all about, meet with no success and the tourists just shake their heads at me. It is a festival about which we know nothing, but like them, I am drawn in by the sheer magnetism, color, movement, and music of the proceedings.

I take a few pictures with the late 17th Century church, La Iglesia de la Compania as a background. Just opposite the church, also bordering the plaza, is a famous cathedral. According to tradition, this was built on the site of a former Inca palace. Inca stonework is apparent everywhere—several buildings in the city are built on original Inca ruins.

I tear myself away from the proceedings around the plaza and have a look at what the nearby streets hold. The commercialized nature of the shops surprises me—all this in the former Inca capital. You can get almost anything in Cuzco—at a price of course. In the shop windows, I see gold

A Journey through Many Worlds

jewelry, Maglite torches, Victorinox knives, pepper spray and virtually every other commodity one would expect in any First World city.

It is almost dark, and the travel guides advise tourists rather take taxis than walk far at night in Cuzco. Just like central Lima, Cuzco is famous for its pickpockets and more blatant robbers.

Just before I return to the Hostel, I buy fruit, bread and a tin of pilchards for dinner. Early the next morning, Joe makes coffee for both of us as we try to shake off the biting cold from the previous night.

A warm shower in the bathrooms does wonders, and I am driven to buy washing powder to wash my clothes. As Murphy's Law will have it, it starts to rain as soon as I have hung up the clothes to dry, and later I am forced to put on wet clothes.

In a street market, we buy a bag full of vegetables and later that evening, cook ourselves up a storm of soup outside the guest house. The only problem is that Joe's stove is not working so well, and he must continually pump it to keep it running. After a mere 45 minutes battling, our soup is ready, and we go inside to enjoy the fruits of our labor.

It is a cold Sunday, the 30th of June, and it is time to begin a recon of the Cuzco ruins. The road which runs alongside our hostel leads past the church of San Cristobal, built, according to many, on the palace stones of the first Inca, Manco Capac. From here we walk the approximately two kilometers to the impressive citadel of Sacsayhuaman.

This very hill was stormed in 1536 by the Conquistador Juan Pizarro and his cavalry, in response to a rebellion led by Manco Inca. After a day's battle, Juan Pizarro was hit on the head by a stone, a wound which proved fatal. After a bloody fight in which thousands died, Saqsayhuaman was reconquered by the Spanish.

Enormous stones—the largest weighs 361 tons—dominate this citadel which rises above Cuzco. It is almost unbelievable that these stones were cut and packed by human hands, as is

Across the Andes

the case with so many other ruins all over the world, it is only possible to speculate upon the real age of Saqsayhuaman. We take shelter from a sudden downpour in a dilapidated building masquerading as a café. Here we are offered Coca tea which now comes into its own, most certainly helping against the cold.

Once the cloudburst passes, we walk a further two kilometers to Qenqo, a holy cave dating from a time long forgotten, surrounded by an amphitheater.

Tambomachay is a further six kilometers away. The magnificent stone structure has been built upon a natural fountain, and cleansing ceremonies were probably held here.

The late afternoon sun starts to peek through the dark rain clouds, and the lighting effect against the carved masterpieces is unnaturally beautiful, the stone works seem to be alive as their clear streams of water rush down into the bright green vegetation. What happened here, hundreds, or maybe even thousands, of years ago? The mind can only wonder.

We begin our walk back just as the first large rain drops start to fall. In my thoughts, I review the spectacular, and almost unbelievable scenes I have just witnessed, and only later do I drift back into reality as the intense cold, driven by a biting wind, brings me back to earth with a jolt.

Back at the hotel, we take a shower and a homemade meal of hot dogs and coffee. Exhausted, having walked more than 20 kilometers for the day, I collapse into bed.

An early morning in Cuzco is cold, very cold. After leaving our guest house, we walk for the last time down the cobbled streets to the bus depot. From there it is a picturesque 53 kilometers past snow capped mountains to Urubamba.

The next minibus takes us 19 kilometers further to Ollantaytambo—one of the few remaining original Inca towns.

On a nearby hill, the formidable fort of Ollantaytambo stands guard, its enormous terraces overshadowing the

A Journey through Many Worlds

town. The Fort forces the passer-by to pay respect as one passes underneath its looming stonework. This very same view greeted the Conquistador Hernando Pizarro in 1536 when he unsuccessfully tried to drive Manco Inca and his followers from the fortress.

When we eventually, and breathlessly, reach the top of the fort, we must stop and rest a while. We have succeeded in climbing the path, the same path that Hernando and his soldiers failed to climb—but they had Incas attacking them as they climbed.

The view from the top is nothing short of fantastic. Seven huge monoliths rise from the citadel. At places, they are covered with fine engraving, on stones each weighing 20 tons and more.

Just imagine how long this work must have taken. And how did they carry these stones all the way up there all those years ago? This is truly a country of many questions and few answers.

Just behind the town is a high mountain which the Incas regarded as holy. In this mountain's features, one is supposed to be able to discern the face of the bearded creator Viracocha. Back in the Inca town; we attempt to stave off the cold with more coffee, brewed on the roadside.

The train—there is no road—to Aguas Calientes only leaves at 20h00 and while we are waiting, a batch of tourists arrive. Stalls next to the small train station sell Coca Tea, and hot corn on the cob served still wrapped in their green leaves.

Chapter 4
Machu Picchu—City of Secrets

"The true mystery of the world is the visible, not the invisible."

— Oscar Wilde

It was in 1991 that the famous explorer and Yale professor, Hiram Bingham, led an expedition to look for what was thought the last Inca capital. During this expedition, he discovered what is today Peru's greatest tourist attraction—Machu Picchu—the 'lost city of the Incas.' Bingham found the city uninhabited and overgrown—a rediscovered treasure which had fortuitously avoided the plundering hand of the Spanish Conquistadors. The rediscovery of Machu Picchu, which means 'Ancient Mountain,' caused a sensation when the National Geographic magazine devoted its entire April 1913 edition to the discovery.

What purpose did this mountain fortress serve?

Did the Incas build it? My deduction is that no-one can say for sure. Even an amateur can see the noticeable difference in building style and construction skills in various parts of the city. To me it is obvious that certain parts have been constructed with tremendous skill and knowledge, while others are of a much more crude style, Bingham also suggested that it was possible that the Incas had built only part of the city, and that other parts could be far older than the Incas themselves.

The most commonly accepted theory is that it was an Inca fortress, built around 500 years ago. There is, however, a significant body of researchers who claim that some parts of

A Journey through Many Worlds

the city are thousands of years older than that.

I suppose it is also true that "generally accepted theories" have also been proven wrong many times in the past. The famous Italian astronomer, physicist, engineer, philosopher and mathematician, Galileo Galilei, said early in the 17th Century that the earth circled the sun, and not the other way round—heresy at the time!

This theory, going strongly against the "generally accepted theory" of the time, led to Galileo being sentenced to life imprisonment, later changed to permanent house arrest!

Our train ride to Aguas Calientes takes almost two hours. The small but busy town, whose name means 'warm waters,' is some 2060 meters above sea level, and is the base from which the daily tourist hordes launch their assault on Machu Picchu. 'Hospedanje Jhon' is located just opposite 'Hospedanje Joe' in a small side street of town. At 10 Soles per person, this fits nicely into our shrinking budget and we book in after a long and demanding day.

The town's lights still shine early the next morning as we cross the bridge over the Urubamba River. There are two ways of seeing Machu Picchu—by foot, or with one of the tourist buses which takes a 30-minute zigzag route up the mountain—at an outrageous price.

We follow a steep gradient stone path through the soft gray clouds and lush green vegetation to the famous destination. We start to climb the many steps. Apparently, some of these stone steps date back to Inca times and a combination of thin air, strenuous exercise and childish excitement makes my heart beat faster and faster.

Reaching the end of the steps about an hour later we are not met by the ancient majestic stone walls which greet us, but a modern hotel with an open air restaurant. It is disappointingly right near the entrance to Machu Picchu. To visit the ruins costs US$ 20 per person, but thanks to our press cards, we get a 50 percent discount.

High above the stone walls of the city, towers the mountain, Huayna Picchu (which means 'young mountain').

Machu Picchu—City of Secrets

From the first place where he gets an overall view of the city, Joe gets his video camera out to start filming.

I decide to walk on further by myself to check out the area before the tourist buses disgorge their human flood. With renewed vigor, I start climbing the terraces to a single building with only three walls, situated on a high point south east of the city. Called the 'Watchman's Post,' it looks out over the so called agricultural section of the city.

It is so amazing to reach this mystical place of which I have read so much about. I remember Joe told me that when he was here 40 years ago, they camped in one of the ruins of the city. There were no other tourists or anybody else around.

Now and then, I stop and take a few pictures. As the moving clouds change the light quality from minute to minute, the whole atmosphere changes before my eyes, and I seem to be unable to stop gaping in wonder.

A French girl snaps me out of my trance by asking me to take a picture of her with Machu Picchu in the background. I do and ask her to return the favor, which she does.

"Photo please!" I hear an Asiatic accent behind me. A nervous looking young Japanese girl waves her camera, giggling all the while. "No problem," I say, and try to take the camera from her. "No, No, No!" she says, and indicates that what she actually wants is a picture of her and me together, which will be taken by her friend.

The picture has scarcely been taken, when she drags me off to Watchman's Post where a whole group of Japanese tourists is standing. This time I must stand in the middle of the group, and pose with a fake smile for a further five pictures before I am allowed to slip away. I don't know if it was my beard or what, but at this stage, I have no real plans to end up in Tokyo, thanks.

I follow the terraces down into the city and enter Machu Picchu through its narrow gate. The paved road leads past a big building on the right-hand side which apparently served as a store.

A Journey through Many Worlds

A little way further on I find the holy plaza with its main temple on the western side and the 'Temple of the Three Windows.' Just to the North West, stairs lead up to the highest point of the city, the so called 'holy hill.' From here, it is thought, the Inca leader would have addressed his followers who would have gathered at the main plaza. Here I also find the Inihuatana, or 'hitching post of the sun.' It is cut out of solid rock and consists of a flat surface with a pointed crown—it could even be a stone replica of Huayna Picchu.

I wonder round in a daze for a few hours, savoring the antiquity of the place. Then I visit the Sun Temple, the Temple of the Condor—and the more I see, the more the desire grows to find out about these ancient part of humanity's history.

Stones, some of which weigh more than 20 tons, fit so neatly on top of each other that they look like giant Lego blocks. There is no cement or other material between the rocks, and the joints are so fine that you cannot put a bank card or a knife between the rocks.

What motivated the builders of this city to create such a titanic project? When dusk starts to settle over the area, I see Joe again for the first time since that morning. A fine rain shower starts as well, and we decide to start the return journey.

The steps down are now slippery and dangerous, so we decide to take the dirt road instead. The more we walk, the harder it rains, and later the path turns into a small river. My poncho is of no more use—I am wet to the core, and even my boots are full of water. Strangely, my spirit for hiking is undaunted—I feel invigorated.

Joe says he feels the same way, and I wonder if it is a result of visiting this city of wonder, Machu Picchu. It is pitch black by the time we hear the sounds of the Urubamba River.

When the rain stops for just a moment, I spot hundreds of green fireflies buzzing in the trees and plants alongside the path. The magical light show is the curtain call of an unforgettable drama which has been today.

Back at Hospedanje Jhon, I take off my wet clothes. My

Machu Picchu—City of Secrets

camera bag is wet, and I anxiously take out the camera and hang the bag up to dry.

Dressed in dry, clean clothes—a polo neck jersey, short pants and a poncho—I set off with Joe in search of food. We find a comfortable looking restaurant. Joe orders the 'Menu Turistico' which consists of a lovely mushroom soup with grated cheese, chicken fillets with rice, chips, and salad, accompanied by Papaya juice.

While we are waiting, the establishment's owner brings us a sought after traditional Peruvian drink—on the house. Pisco Sour is made of Pisco (a sort of brandy), egg white, lemon, and sugar. I think it tastes particularly awful, but Joe remarks that it is "Not bad, not bad at all" after he has gulped his glass away. I go to bed with a full stomach and a mountain range full of memories.

The next day is Wednesday, and we decide that it is a day of rest. We will try to get our clothes and camera bags dry and sort out the other equipment. At the end of the day, all is acceptably dry, and we get an early night's rest.

It is still dark the next morning at 05h00 when we start walking towards the station to catch the train back to Ollantaytambo.

Near the station, I slip in the muddy path and fall backward onto my rucksack in the middle of the road, much to the amusement of some Peruvians behind me. On the train, images of the 'Inca City' flash through my mind. "There are so many questions, and so few answers"—this is fast becoming my mantra.

Chapter 5
Walking on Water—
Journey to the Lake in the Clouds

"All the great Legends are Templates for human behavior. I would define a myth as a story that has survived"

—John Boorman

At the beginning of time, says the Inca legend, there was a great god called Viracocha. He created a world totally shrouded in darkness. Then he created humankind, and for a while, everything went well in this dark world. However, man sinned against Viracocha and was therefore severely punished. The heavens opened, and it rained for 60 days and 60 nights and as mighty waters covered the land, everything, including man, perished.

After this mighty flood, Viracocha decided on a new creation. He went to an island on Lake Titicaca from which he flung the sun, the moon, and the stars into the heavens. The moon was brighter than the sun in those days, and the sun was very jealous. Therefore the sun took some ashes and threw it across the face of the moon. By looking at the moon, one can even today still see the evidence!

Viracocha created humankind again and ordered them to populate the land. The Sun sent his son, Manco Capac, the first Inca, and the Moon her daughter, Mama Occlo to the waters of Lake Titicaca. Manco Capac had in his hand a golden staff, and they were ordered to wander the land in search of a fertile place to settle.

Searching for many years, they came at the base of a mountain called Huanacauri. There they saw a rainbow in

Walking on Water

the sky. Manco Capac said it was a good omen, explaining that it is a sign to show that the earth will never be destroyed by water again. When they arrived at the present valley of Cuzco, at a place called Huanay-Pata, the golden staff sunk into the ground and they knew the soil was fertile. It was here that the great Inca capital of Cuzco would arise.

Viracocha, meaning "sea foam," has been described as being a bearded man of white skin color who had blue eyes. He is said to have disappeared, moving east across the ocean, with a promise to return one day. Some say that when the Spanish conquistador Francisco Pizarro and his band of 181 soldiers marched into South America and the Inca Empire on the 16th of November 1532, the locals saw it as the return of Viracocha.

The white men arrived in the same way the Inca god departed—across the water. However, these 181 "gods" would soon bring the mighty Inca Empire of millions to a fall.

The Spanish politely invited the Inca ruler, Atahualpa, to meet with them at Cajamarca, Peru. At the meeting place, Pizarro's men ambushed and attacked the mass of Indians. In the ensuing battle, the 181 soldiers, armed with rifles and swords, killed thousands of natives and captured their leader.

Pizarro promised Atahualpa that he would release him if he ordered his subjects to fill one entire room with golden artifacts and another two with silver. For months and from all over the Empire, gold and silver were carried to Cajamarca. This being completed, the Inca asked to be released. Next, Pizarro ordered the execution of the Inca Emperor, Atahualpa

Atahualpa then said "'What have I done, or my children, that I should meet such a fate? And from your hands, too, you, who I have met with friendship and kindness from my people, with whom I have shared my treasures, who have received nothing but benefits from my hands!'

Just before sunset by the end of August 1533, Atahualpa was

A Journey through Many Worlds

prepared to be burned. Friar Valverde then offered another option of how he can be killed—by garrote (strangulation) if the Inca leader agrees to be baptized.

Atahualpa agrees and he dies by the hands of the Spanish. Francisco Pizarro and his soldiers then started their march towards the legendary Inca capital of Cuzco which was then inhabited by around 150 000 people. The city was laid out in the form of a jaguar. The Jaguar (meaning "he who kills with one blow") was worshiped by the Incas, Mayans and Aztecs in some way.

The Cuzco bus depot is chaos. Tourists from the four corners of the earth stand around in groups. Inside the building, bus agencies and their operatives rattle off the names of destinations: "Puno, Puno, Punoooo....Arequipa, Arequipa, Arequipaaaa." The shrill voices and the monotonous repetition is enough to drive anyone off their head.

Our plan is to visit Puno as the next stop on our tour, and after another round of negotiations, the price of the ticket drops from 50 Soles per person to a mere 13 Soles. The bus leaves after one of the passenger load an entire bedroom's furniture onto the roof. Fortunately it is a tar road, and I managed to catch a bit of shut eye on the trip. Joe, however, has difficulty sleeping in a moving vehicle, but thanks to my experience in the South African Army, this is an art I mastered many years ago.

The vegetation slowly changes into wide open grass plains, and six hours later, we arrive in Puno, with its city lights reflecting off the still waters of Lake Titicaca. At 3 800 meters (12 500 feet) above sea level, Titicaca is the highest navigable lake in the world, with a surface area of 8 288 square kilometers. It is also the biggest lake in South America with no less than 25 rivers feeding the lake. The deepest point measured to date in the lake is 280 meters. It borders Bolivia, and Peru, and contains more than 40 islands, of which some are inhabited.

The somewhat eccentric explorer Graham Hancock wrote in his book, 'Fingerprints of the Gods' that there are in the

Walking on Water

Titicaca area, many fossilized sea shells to be found, and that particular types of sea horses have been found there as well. This would indicate that the region once was a sea which has been forced to its present altitude by large seismic forces. In this way, a piece of the sea has been captured at the top of Andes.

The Hostel Margarita is a neat and clean place with hot water, a friendly service, clean bed clothes, bed lamps and even a toilet seat. I cannot believe my luck—this is, I have long since discovered, a real rare find in the Andes. The next morning we take a red three wheel cycle power taxi to the harbor, in search of transport which will take us to an exotic tribe of Indians who live on one of the lake's islands. We find a motor boat to take us out, and a half hour later, we can see the yellow outline of the Uros islands in the distance.

The Uros tribe are known as the 'reed people' and for a good reason: not only do they live in reed huts on manmade reed islands, but their mode of transport is reed boats, and they even eat reeds. There is not very much more that one can think of that they do not do with reeds.

The Uros islands had their origin several hundred years ago thanks to the Inca Empire's sudden expansion. The Uros wanted to remain independent and created their new homeland on the lake. Totora, which is plentiful in the lake, was packed in layers and the islands formed. Every few weeks they pack more reeds on top, as the ones at the bottom rot away. In this way, these people have been continuously building their islands for around 500 years.

We are invited to sleep over on one of the smaller islands for the night, and a family evacuates their hut to provide us with a bedroom. Walking on these islands is a strange sensation. The reeds give way with each step, creating the feeling of walking on a huge waterbed. It is dark in the hut— there are no windows. Joe switches on his Petzl head lamp and closes the door, which of course is also made of reeds. As my eyes adjust to the darkness, I see our bed: a pack of reeds, about the size of a double bed.

In one corner of the single roomed hut, stands a brand

47

A Journey through Many Worlds

new, unconnected, porcelain toilet. As it is not connected, I presume it is used as a chair. Clothes are scattered around on the floor, and on the other side of the bed is a broad wooden set of shelves, containing an array of items I did not expect. There is an American 'Super Slicer,' still wrapped in plastic, proudly displaying its 'As seen on TV' sticker, and a Silver Hi-Fi set. Unfortunately, the electrical items can only be used during the day as the power source is a solar panel mounted on a pole alongside the hut.

Reed people and solar panels. I shake my head at the contrast. The wind, which started to blow a little earlier, has now reached a few degrees below storm strength, and we decided to reconnoiter the island further in the morning.

Now I notice that it is extremely cold in the hut, and after making my diary entry for the day, I crawl into my sleeping bag and try to get to sleep, trying to convince myself that it's not really a few degrees below freezing. Every weekday morning, the children from these floating islands row, in their reed boats, to the main island to attend classes in a reed school. These boats consist of bundles of totora bound together with rope. Some of them have faces painted on their bows, which reminds one of Viking ships. The rowing team is mounted at the rear of the craft and the boat is propelled forward with a sort of 'figure of eight' motion.

But today is Saturday, and our host, Oscar, orders his eight-year-old son to take me out onto the lake on his totora boat. I follow the child, who with a sigh of protest, begins to slowly drag himself off in the direction of a few boats tied up together. The three-meter reed boat is not very stable, and I sit dead quiet while my young chauffeur starts rowing in the direction of their fishing nets. Once arrived, he pulls up the nets, only to discover that the single catch is one 10 centimeter fish in the entire net.

Back on the island, breakfast is served. This consists of fish (not the 10-centimetre job, but something more substantial), rice and potato. The meal is prepared on an open fire, mounted on a flat stone. After breakfast, I stroll around to see what else is happening on this strange island.

48

Walking on Water

Alongside one of the other huts, I find a young boy holding up what appears to be a wind shield. Sheltering behind this shield is a small girl, frenetically grinding up corn between two stones. If her brother does not hold up the shield, the wind will blow the fruits of her labor away.

Not far away a man is busy cutting new reeds. He uses a long stick with a blade set at a 90-degree angle to cut the stem under the water. It is quite incredible to think of how these people have adapted to life on the water. Once we have packed up and thanked the islanders for their wonderful hospitality, Oscar takes us on one of the bigger boats to the main island, where a motor boat will take us back to Puno.

It is time to move on, and back at the bus depot, we buy tickets -10 Soles each—to Arequipa. The next bus leaves at 20h00, and this means we have a six-hour wait. At 03h00, the Romeliza bus arrives in a rather chilly Arequipa. In that town's bus depot, the rows of chairs are full of sleeping people, and we decide to follow their example. I put my rucksack down in front of my chair, rest my head on it and in a few minutes, I am fast asleep.

The Conquistador Francisco Pizarro founded Arequipa in 1540, and for reasons best known to him, the site is at the foot of the slumbering volcano, El Misti (the Gentleman). As a result, many of Arequipa's buildings are built of sillar, a white volcanic stone, giving rise to Arequipa's nick name, the 'White City.'

With a population of more than 725,000, Arequipa is also the second largest city in Peru. At about 06h00, we catch a taxi to the Hostel Regi. I climb onto the guest house's roof to watch the sun dawn, shootings its majestic rays out from behind the snow covered El Misti. It is a glorious sight. After a stiff cup of coffee, I venture into the surrounding streets. The first thing I notice is that Arequipa has to be the cleanest city in all of Peru. It is Sunday, and on the plaza, soldiers from several different sections of the army are carrying out what appears to be a drill parade. I don't see any tourists and wonder if the riots and violence of a few weeks ago are the possible reason for this show of force.

49

A Journey through Many Worlds

A visit to the market is another exciting experience, and most unusual are the wide variety of potatoes on sale: different colors, sizes and shapes galore. Then I am reminded that Peru's greatest gift to the world is the potato. I can now see why. The nunnery of Santa Catalina is another famous spot I heard of. It was built as a 'city within a city' in 1580, and around 450 nuns lived here—in relays of course—for more than 400 years, completely isolated from the outside world. Today a large part of Santa Catalina is open to the public, and I can recommend a visit there for anyone wishing to have an experience as close to life as possible of Medieval times.

The Medieval Age has fortunately long gone, and today is Monday, 8 July 2002. We have been in Peru for almost a month, and I feel like I have been here years already. Our bus to Nazca which should have left at a quarter to twelve only leaves at quarter past one, but we are not fazed. The trip to the sea takes us through a desert landscape, complete with mini dunes. The West Coast mist which we first experienced in Lima greets us once again as we reach the coast at Camana. It appears deserted and neglected.

The Pasifico del Sur bus' seats are harder than church pews, and we are grateful to disembark at the small town of Nazca some nine hours later.

50

Chapter 6
Nazca—Sketchbook of the Ancients

"There are Mysteries which men can only guess at, which age by age they may solve only in part"

—Bram Stoker

The taxi drivers waiting for us at the bus depot in Nazca is anxious to get our attention. Two women in an old white Mercedes finally win this right after they offer us accommodation in the hostel 'Estrella del Sur' (Southern Star) at 10 Soles. This includes the Taxi and breakfast. Our suspicions as to what exactly this breakfast might be, are allayed: it is two rolls, butter, jam, and tea. Not bad. Alongside the table is the hostel's mascot, a wooly white dog with the appropriate name of Estrellita—little star.

Joe and I discuss our plans for the next two days at Nazca. A flight over the famous Nazca lines as well as a visit to the nearby Chauchilla graveyard are the major objectives of our visit to this little desert town. We take a taxi to the local airfield where we find numerous companies offering flights over the Nazca lines —at prices which vary between US$ 35 and US$ 200 per person. Armed with this information, we decide to go for a flight the next day and we return to the hostel. A combined chicken and spaghetti dish at 5 Soles is on offer at the local 'Chifa' (Asian restaurant), and once we gulp this acceptable meal down, we set off for the Chauchilla graveyards.

Carlos, the taxi driver, drives like a maniac and our adventure nearly comes to an ironically fitting end in the graveyard, when he finally loses control of the vehicle. The taxi slides across the road on a corner, narrowly missing a

A Journey through Many Worlds

truck coming from the opposite direction. Obviously, a little bit shaken by the dramatically close shave, Carlos calms down a bit and the last two kilometers to our destination are taken at a leisurely pace, with the taxi driver telling us with relish about how he robbed graves in the area as a youngster.

The Chauchilla graveyard is eerie, to say the least. Whitened human bones lay scattered around the dry desert floor in every direction for almost as far as one can see. Here and there a few screens have been put up over the entombed graves in which mummies sit, singly and in groups, waiting for the sun to rise in the East. The late midday sun emphasizes the red hair which many of the mummies have, and I am forced to think about the legends of the red haired people of Easter Island. Is there possibly a connection?

This desert region on the coast of Peru is one of the driest places on earth. It only rains for a few minutes each year, and it is this phenomenon to which the mummies—around 2000 years old—owe their existence.

In some of the tombs, the mummies have been found with pots and other articles, but sadly as a result of the activities of people such as our taxi driver Carlos, a vast amount of historical clues have been destroyed by tomb robbers over the centuries. There is also a high demand by short sighted 'private collectors' who buy these items from the locals.

After a good night's rest, we return to the Aero Paracas agency at the airfield. Typically for aerial photography, I use an aircraft that has its door removed, but for some reason, Raul, the pilot of this plane, is not so keen on my idea. The young pilot from the Tingo Maria region is however eventually persuaded to allow me to open the window of the Cessna 172 during the flight—a task which I accomplish with the aid of my Leatherman. I am however grateful to Raul for his assistance, as pictures taken through a glass window are nearly always distorted and refracted.

In the 1920s, passengers on board commercial flights over the Nazca plains reported seeing lines which reminded them of landing strips. The first real research into the lines was undertaken by the American Paul Kosok, who later joined up

Nazca—Sketchbook of the Ancients

with the German scientist Maria Reiche. They believed that the lines formed part of a giant calendar which might have had some agricultural purpose.

Apart from the around 800 lines which stretch over the desert floor (some of which are several kilometers in length), there are also several sketches of animals, plants and even people etched out on this massive drawing book. These 'lines,' or geoglyphs, have been made by removing the dark colored stones on the surface, thereby exposing the lighter colored layer underneath. As there is almost no surface wind and pathetically little rain, these lines have remained pristine for about the last 2000 years.

Kosok died in 1959, and Maria Reiche, 'The lady of the lines,' devoted the rest of her life to studying and researching the lines. In 1968, an American astronomer, Gerald S Hawkins, went to Nazca to try and determine with the aid of early computer projections if the lines could have been used as an astronomical calendar. His findings were however negative.

At ground level, one cannot even see the lines, and it is only from the air that one gets perspective on this giant sketchpad. This aerial bound view of the lines gripped a man by the name of Jim Woodman, a writer, and publisher in Miami, who developed a theory that the Nazca people must have been able to fly for these lines to have any meaning.

It was Woodman, who famously in 1975 tried to prove his theory by making a hot air balloon out of fine woven linen—similar to that recovered from archaeological digs at Nazca. His hot air balloon, Condor 1, actually did fly on 28 November 1975, rising to a height of 300 foot above sea level before descending once again.

It remains an interesting theory, but no conclusive evidence has ever been shown that the Nazcas were so advanced that they knew how to fly. At least, it seems more plausible than other more bizarre theories have included a supposition that the lines are markers for interplanetary travelers.

A Journey through Many Worlds

But still, the question remains: why did they make these massive pictures in the desert, and who was meant to see them, except from the air? The Gods? In March 1972, the unmanned interplanetary Pioneer 10 was launched from Cape Kennedy, Florida. The purpose of this mission was to explore the furthermost reaches of the solar system and beyond, and it was the first ship ever to leave our solar system, a feat accomplished in 1983.

In January 2003, NASA received the last signal from Pioneer 10, some 12.3 billion kilometers from earth and heading in the direction of the star Aldebaran, in the constellation of Taurus, the bull. On board that ship is a message on behalf of humanity to any other intelligent form of life. A gold plated aluminum tablet with a picture of a man and woman, and a picture of the ship itself. It also contains other coded information about the earth's location and proximity to other planets. If all goes according to plan, says NASA, Pioneer 10 should reach Aldebaran in 2 million years or so . . . And herein lays the parallel with the Nazca lines: what if the plate on Pioneer 10 has the same meaning as the Nazca lines? Does the possibility not exist that they are a message that there is intelligent life elsewhere?

"On your left-hand side you can see the Hummingbird and then we will bank right towards the Spider," shouts Raul over the drone of the engine as he whips the small craft around like a toy. Joe is white in the face. Flying in a Cessna is obviously not one of his favorite pastimes, and I can see in his eyes that the history of the lines is one of the last, if not the last, thing on his mind right now. Maybe only food is lower down than the Nazca lines in Joe's mind. Some 35 minutes later, a thankful Joe and I can emerge from the Cessna and get into a distinctly earthly taxi. Later in the afternoon, Juan, a taxi driver, shows me a batch of pictures of skulls set out on display in a hut.

He takes us to a local woman's house and in her backyard is a small room where the remains of more than 30 people are on display. In between the skulls lie bits of finely woven material and pottery shards. A huge sandal attracts my attention, and Juan explains, almost nonchalantly, that,

54

Nazca—Sketchbook of the Ancients

oh yes, long ago, giants lived in Nazca as well. According to Juan, everything on display in the room was picked up locally, and it is clear that the woman keeps this collection for private profit—we had to pay 5 Soles for the privilege of viewing it. Just a few meters away a woman sits in the garden, undisturbed by our presence, playing cards with a friend while a few chickens peck around in the background.

Our tour of Peru is coming to an end, and the next day we will leave on a bus back to Lima. By now a lot fitter than when we left Lima, we walk the approximately seven kilometers from the bus stop to Rhodas 1—in the rain. After a good cup of coffee and a hot shower, Joe retires to bed. I find Roxanna and her brother Alex in the lounge in front of the TV, and over a glass or seven of Aguardiente, ('firewater') I start trying to improve my Spanish. Roxanna gets this colorless homemade alcohol from her parents who live in the jungle, and it is made from sugar cane. Its alcohol content is around 70%, and that combined with a strong molasses aftertaste makes it compulsory for non-Indians to mix it with coke or something, to prevent instant memory loss or worse.

A little later in the evening, I am convinced that I can speak better Spanish than English, and I decide that at this stage it is probably wisest for me to go to bed. The next morning it is Saturday 13 July, and it is precisely a month since we left South Africa. I cannot believe how quickly the time has flown, yet at the same time, it feels as if I have been in Peru for years. The first part of the journey is now over, and from here we will enter the Amazon basin—another world where there are no crowds of tourists, buses with TVs, etc.

We get front row, top deck seats on the Mercedes bus to Tingo Maria, and are afforded a 'big screen' view of the passing scenery. After about 11 hours on board the luxury coach, we are taken over the Andes Mountains and reach Abra de Anticona, at the height of 15,890 feet above sea level. We are now on the world's highest tarred road, and next stop on our route is La Oroya. The first settlement here dates back to 10 000 years BC, and it is today an important mining town.

Chapter 7
Entering the River World of the Amazon Jungle

"The forest is a peculiar organism of unlimited kindness and benevolence that makes no demands for its sustenance and extends generously the products of its life and activity; it affords protection to all beings."

—Buddist Sutra

The Amazon River (Rio Amazonas) has its origin some 17 000 feet (over 5000 meters) above sea level in the snow capped Andes Mountains in Peru, near to the South American west coast.

From there, it wanders nearly 7000 kilometers, ending in the Atlantic Ocean on the East Coast of the continent. It is the largest river on earth: its catchment area is roughly as big as Australia, and it crosses several country borders.

This giant river pumps on average between 34 and 121 million liters of water every second. In one day the river discharges about the same volume of water as the river Thames does in one year. It transports more water than the next eight largest rivers in the world combined and during the wet season areas of the river can be more than 190 kilometers (120 miles) wide! More than 1100 tributaries feed the main river, and it contains 20 percent of Earth's freshwater. When it reaches the Atlantic, it has generated so much pressure that fresh water extends for several hundred

Entering the River World

kilometers into the ocean.

The average depth of the Amazon River is between 20 and 50 meters (66 to 164 ft) but in some places up to 100 meters (330 ft). At the height of the rainy season; it is 50 kilometers wide in places. There are hundreds of islands in the river. At its mouth, Marajó, it is more than 36,000 km in surface area, bigger than Belgium. At Iquitos in Peru, 3600 kilometers from the Atlantic Ocean, at low water season, the river is only 100 meters above sea level. This means that the river drops in altitude only by some 2 centimeters (less than an inch) per kilometer.

The more than 5600 fish species as recorded in the Amazon dwarf the mere 522 species in European rivers and is also in excess of all the fish species found in the Atlantic Ocean itself! On a single tree in Peru, more than 43 different species of ant have been found—nearly as many as in the entire UK. The bio-diversity wonders of the South American rainforest are a series of miracles on their own.

The Amazon rain forests have often been described as the 'lungs of the earth' because of the forest's massive task of converting an estimated 500 million tons of carbon dioxide each year into oxygen. Around one fifth of the world's oxygen is produced by the South American rain forest. It is already dark when we reach the small town of Tingo Maria, nestling in the depths of the Huallaga Valley. We are now at the edge of the Amazon and have dropped to 2000 feet above sea level. Tingo Maria is a mainly Quechua speaking town of about 5000 families.

The town's economy is agricultural, and more specifically the production of Coca. Drug related violence has caused many inhabitants to flee the area. The American Drug Enforcement Administration (DEA), FBI and the Peruvian Army regularly launch full-scale operations against the drug trade in the region. While we are waiting for our bus driver to open the baggage compartment of our bus, I hear the familiar sound of a helicopter above me. From our position inside the bus depot, we cannot see anything, but the next minute a few shots ring out in the distance. Instinct takes over, and I am

A Journey through Many Worlds

overcome by a desire to get closer to the ground.

The bus driver and other locals seem completely undisturbed and carry on with their tasks as if shootouts are an ordinary event. I guess it may be normal around here, but I wonder for a moment if they do not mind being shot?

As the disturbing noise dies down, we summon a red three wheel motorcycle taxi to take us to the Hotel 'Palacio,' an old colonial building with a huge entrance hall where beautiful exotic animals are kept in the most shockingly awful cages. For the first time, I feel like I am in the tropics. The hot air is heavy with the humidity and contrasts sharply with the icy Andes air which we breathed earlier that day.

On Sunday 14th July, Joe goes off to visit some nearby caves while I head off to try and find an Internet café in town to sort out some issues. Oilbirds, also called Guacharos, are found in these caves. They are related to Nighthawks, and like bats, stay in the caves during the day. They live on palm nuts and navigate in the pitch blackness with the aid of an echolocation system, similar to sonar. They have their name thanks to the Indians who catch and cook the little Oilbirds to extract smokeless oil from them, which is then used in cooking.

It is early in the morning when a taxi takes us to the bus company. The next bus leaves at 11:00 and the trip to Pucallpa cost 15 Soles. While we're waiting, three UH-1 Huey helicopter gunships sweep low over the town. They are painted olive green, and I can see heavily armed personnel through the open side doors. The Hueys circle a few times, their rotors pulsating that typical action packed "Vietnam" movie adrenalin and then disappear against the backdrop of the mountain, La Bella Durmiente—the sleeping beauty.

What will this jungle phase of our adventure hold in store?

The road to Pucallpa is in places extremely poor. A recent landslide has left parts of the road almost unusable. Around one of the bends, we find another bus which has become stuck and our drivers stop to pick up the stranded passengers. After an uncomfortable ride on the Trans-Andean highway,

Entering the River World

we enter the busy frontier town at 20h00. The streets are full of hooting brightly colored two-stroke three wheeled taxis racing here there and everywhere, creating the distinct impression that there are more taxis than pedestrians. We book in at the Hostel 'Sun' for a mere 20 Soles per person.

An overweight lady armed with suspicious fast moving eyes gives Joe the key to our grimy first-floor room. It is equipped with a roof fan and no windows. Maybe it is better that way, as Pucallpa is quite literally a stinking city. The furniture consists of two single beds and an old wooden cupboard.

Farther down the hall are the communal bathrooms and toilets without seats. There are only cold water taps, as here, hot water appears to be completely unnecessary. Pucallpa is on the banks of the Ucayali River, which is one of the headwaters of the Amazon River.

From here we must get a river boat to where the Sheshea River empties into the Ucayali. After this, the plan is then to move up the Sheshea to a place indicated as "San Gregorio" on our map. From there again we must, in some manner yet to be determined, get to the town of Puerto Portillo, which is next to the origin of the Jurua River—our ultimate prize.

Right now, however, our priority is to find out where we can get a boat to the mouth of the Sheshea. There seems to be an ants' nest of boats on the banks of the Ucayali. Tree stumps and worked wood alike are loaded on and off the different boats ad infinitum.

Stalls made of timber and plastic lines the river bank and everything can be bought here—from wire, beer, fish hooks to condoms. In the water itself, dozens of old, heavily used boats and many canoes bob around. Some of the bigger boats display a list of their destinations, and time of departure hastily scribbled on a dirty plastic container.

Surveying this chaos, Joe suggests that we first get all our supplies together and then only come back to decide on a boat. We walk back to the hostel. I mentioned that Pucallpa stinks. And yes it is also dirty. Very dirty. In one side street

A Journey through Many Worlds

a few kids kick around a soccer ball, while only a few short meters away, black vultures and skinny dogs fight each other for a pile of rotting barber fish heads. Trash lies everywhere, and the stink of decay combined with diesel fumes leave an indelible impression upon me. Joe and I begin to patrol the town in search of the last bit of equipment we will need for the trip up the river.

Pucallpa is the last large town which we expect to see for the next few months. We buy machetes, a grinding stone, a kettle, a pan, hammocks and a mosquito net. We will only buy food just before we leave. Fortunately the shops of Pucallpa stock almost everything. The only item I fail to get is a thermometer. I have lost mine on one of the buses during the Andes phase of our journey.

Back in Pucallpa's harbor, I set the Pentax up on a tripod and take a few pictures of myself and Joe. I get the film developed at a laboratory in town, and by a large fortune I find an Internet café which I use to scan and email the photos to Arthur back in South Africa. He has set up a website about our trip and will use the photos for that as well as send them to the newspaper in my hometown, the Paarl Post.

We stroll around looking for food supplies. Everywhere in the town we find stalls selling fruit: water melon, apples, bananas, mangos, and avocados are aplenty and also, other tropical fruit about, the likes of which I have never seen before, but which taste delicious.

My favorite is Chirimoya—a lovely tasting round fruit which cannot be compared to anything else. At the pharmacy or Farmacia, opposite the hostel, I find a scale and weigh myself for the first time since leaving South Africa. Then I weighed some 72 kilograms, and now I see I am 66 kilograms but feel much healthier than I did when we first arrived in South America.

I telephone a friend from the hostel, and it sounds strange to hear another familiar voice again. I do not know when next I will get to a phone or have internet access again. Near to Pucallpa lies an oxbow lake named Yarina Cocha.

60

Entering the River World

We hire a small wooden boat to take us out to the Cabana, where there are many different sorts of animals and birds to be seen. During this trip, I see for the first time a freshwater dolphin. The gray dolphin called bufeo or tucuxi (Sotalia fluviatilis) is one of the two species of dolphin one encounters in the Amazon.

He closely resembles his salt water cousins and grows to a length of about 1.5 meters. At the Cabana, we tie our boat up as a middle aged man walks up to greet us. He offers to show us around, and a few meters further we see a three toed sloth busy munching on leaves in a tree.

This animal has a flat head with big, friendly eyes and a dumb expression, and evokes pity in me. Three-toed sloths spend at least 80 percent of their lives sleeping or resting, hanging upside down on a branch. They spend so much time hanging upside down; their hair grows from the stomach to their backs to allow rain to wash off them with ease.

They remind me of the speed of consumer service back in South Africa, and when they are threatened, the sloth races off at a death defying 4.5 meters per minute. At this speed, it is highly difficult to escape very many enemies, and as a result, the sloth makes more use of camouflage as a means of protection.

Sloths are also too lazy to wash, and the green algae which grow on the coats help to merge them into the rain forest background.

Another interesting animal which we meet is the world's largest rodent, the capybara or carpincho. It looks like a guinea pig on steroids, is about 1.4 meters long and weighs more than 50 kilograms.

With its webbed feet, a carpincho is at home in the water as it is in a swamp. It is often tamed—and sometimes eaten— by the locals.

A Boa Constrictor lies lazily in the grass. These snakes can reach several meters in length and are not poisonous at all— they kill their prey by squeezing their victims to death. With their unlockable jaws, they can swallow prey many times

A Journey through Many Worlds

larger than themselves. In such a case, they then lay down for weeks at a time, slowly digesting their super meal. It is time to go back.

After a refreshing local beer at the Cabana, we get back into our motor boat and leave. It is now Wednesday the 24th of July, and we are eventually ready to go to Pucallpa.

My attempt to draw some money at the Interbank has proven fruitless, and the manager helpfully explains that there is no money in their ATM anyway. According to him, the ATM might be fixed later, but he cannot say for sure when. But those who persevere win, and after a while, I can withdraw 250 Soles.

We buy 150 Soles worth of food, which includes lentils, beans, flour, carrots, onions, potatoes, salt, sugar, and chilies. We also buy a few luxuries like Worcestershire Sauce, soya sauce, chili sauce and few tins of food and tinned butter.

A taxi in the form of a station wagon—in Europe they call them estates—takes us to the harbor while a group of screaming youngsters runs behind us. They are all aspirant porters, and the lack of tourists makes competition particularly stiff. 'Transportes Rios' is the name of the boat we have chosen to take us to the mouth of the Sheshea. It is the best we can find, but even so, it is a dirty and neglected steel hulled wreck masquerading as a seaworthy vessel. On the top deck is a large sign with the departure time: '17h00 Sin Falta'—which means 17h00 'without fail.'

17h00 comes and goes. We are already at ease below deck, which is an open space about eight by 3.5 meters. It is big enough to hang your hammock almost anywhere. To the rear of the boat are two small room like structures opposite each other—the toilet and the kitchen and in the corner of the former, three chickens are bundled closely together...

If you walk through the narrow passage between this lot, you get to a small platform at the rear—an open air bathroom. An old rusted five-liter paint bucket with a long rope attached to it is tied to the rail. A bath takes place this way: you throw the bucket overboard and pull up some river

Entering the River World

water in which to wash. You have to be a bit careful while you do this because the exposed steel rod which controls the boat's rudder runs directly under your feet.

There is still no other passengers or baggage, and it becomes painfully clear that we will not leave tonight at all. Later one of the crew offers us supper, but even in the dull light the food looks appalling, and we decline the generous offer. After a few rounds of cards, we decide to catch some shut eye. My first night in a hammock I find cool and very restful.

Chapter 8
Up the Ucayali—Headwater of the Amazon

"I believe that the earthly Paradise lies here, which no one can enter except by God's leave. I believe that this land which your Highnesses have commanded me to discover is very great and that there are many other areas in the south of which there have never been reports."

—Christopher Columbus

Thursday, quarter past seven PM, exactly 26 hours and fifteen minutes behind schedule, we leave. "Sin Falta" Sure... The passenger total has grown to about 15 and baggage of all sorts crowds every nook and cranny of the boat. We have to work our way between bottles of water, soft drinks, maize, sugar, bananas and personal belongings, all of which crowds the gangways. Some of the passengers are traders who vend their goods at the smaller villages further along the river.

On the top deck a nice cool breeze can be felt, almost daring us to come on as we chug slowly upstream against the Ucayali. Eventually, we are on the river itself, and both Joe and I are silent.

When I later fall asleep in my hammock, the last thing I hear is the uneven drone of the Transportes Rios. At 01h00 I wake up. Something is wrong—the boat's engines are silent. According to the moon's position, we are drifting along with the rivers current! Then orders are shouted in Spanish, and through the darkness, I discern that we are slowly drifting

64

Up the Ucayali

towards the river bank. Oh Shit, I think to myself, but still just turn over and go back to sleep.

The following day we spend tied up against the river bank while the crew tries to repair the engine. It's apparent that they don't know what the problem is, so it is pointless to even ask. One moment the captain tells us that we will be on our way again shortly, and then the next he tells us that he has called for help by radio and that we must wait. Shit. As if we have other options!

I decide that this is the ideal opportunity to try and catch some fish. This is a first for me, as I have never fished before in my life. The boat's kitchen gives me a piece of meat to use as bait, and after a few hours in the baking tropical sun, I boast a batch of eight Barber type fish as my booty. Later I visit the toilet and find only two traumatized chickens left in the corner of the small dirty cabin. Their dearly departed travel mate is, of course, on the menu today...

A woman, who serves as the cook on board, prepares the fish for us, along with a slightly less pleasant baked banana. Joe and I polish off three fish and then give the rest of the haul to a very grateful crew.

"Muito Obrigado!", They reply with broad smiles, and I wonder why they don't catch fish themselves ... Saturday 27th comes and goes, and we are still stranded in a broken boat on the riverbank. Some of the crew and passengers disembark and head off in the direction of a banana plantation. A while later, one of them returns. He is a man of about 50 years old, and he asks Joe and me to come with him. Joe is however too busy reading his dictionary and is not interested.

But of course, I want to go! I grab my camera, and we walk down the narrow wooden gangplank to the riverside. A narrow path winds its way through the shock green banana plantation and runs past two huts standing next to each other. They are Indian huts, decked with palm leaves. About seven adults and what seems to be a swarm of children wait for us in the huts, and it crosses my mind that visitors must be rare—I wonder what they are thinking.

65

A Journey through Many Worlds

"Ah! Gringo!", I am greeted.

In Central and South America, Westerners are called like this. There is a story which says that the word had its origin when Mexicans heard American soldiers singing "Green grow the rushes, O" but the more likely explanation is the Spanish word for Greek is "Griego"—and that in Spanish, as is the case in English and Afrikaans, when something is difficult to understand, it is referred to as 'Greek.' Thus one can conclude that the Spanish speaking population of Central and South America must view the English speakers as "Greeks."

The Gringo is called closer. Everyone appears to be in a cheerful mood, most likely thanks to an empty bottle with a pungent alcoholic odor lying abandoned to one side. It is interesting to watch these people drink. A small amount of alcohol is poured into a glass. The bottle is then passed to the next person, while the poured alcohol is gulped down in one quick swig. The next one in line does the same thing and passes the glass on once again. And so the process continues, and the bottle might do a few rounds until it is empty. To pour yourself a full glass when it is your turn is unforgivable and downright rude in this jungle.

It looks like they have called me from the boat to have an excuse to drink. A new bottle is opened, and I begin the round with a clean glass. When the glass reaches me again, I indicate that I have had enough. Fourteen eyes look at me with disappointment etched in their irises, but I really cannot bring myself to share a glass with the entire jungle...

Without saying anything, a woman appears and gives me a bottle containing a dark liquid. It is mine, she indicates. For a moment I am silly enough to think this is coca-cola. With everyone watching me, I take a sip. Holy shit—this is BAD! But the second swig is not quite as bad as the first.

"Bom?" asks a man wearing a severely bleached Batman cap, while he holds his thumb up. 'Si! Bom!", I lie, with a forced smile. After I have nearly finished the glass, the neat Aguardiente does start to taste even better.

66

Up the Ucayali

"Muito problemo!", I jokingly point towards the glass. They apparently misunderstand me, because, while some laugh, the woman appears with a new drink. For a second I don't think I am going to get out of here conscious.

Fortunately the drinking session ends, and we are fed a lovely meal from the hut alongside, prepared and served by a young Indian girl. Barbecued fish, Yucca (a type of root) and bananas.

After the meal I take a few pictures and then one of the crew arrives to call us back to the boat. Joe is still lying in his hammock. He peers at me from over his glasses but says nothing. It is probably better.

In spite of the food, I feel distinctly light headed and head for the toilet again. The last chicken seems to have made peace with the inevitable. He is sitting in the corner with a faraway look, waiting to be served. Chicken a la toilet it will be. Suddenly I am more grateful than ever I ate on dry land.

At midday, the Transportes Rios gets underway once again, and I decide it is opportune to have a little afternoon snooze in my hammock.

I quickly slip into welcome unconsciousness, and when I emerge once again, it is dark and has been so for an evidently long time. I go up to the upper deck and find Joe there. The moon is almost full and busy rising in the east. Now and then the boat's crew switch on a spotlight to watch out for trees, branches, or other bits of potentially dangerous flotsam which might damage the vessel's hull. Sometimes the spotlight crosses the river banks, and we see dozens of red eyes reflected back at us.

"Jacare," explains the captain. They are black caiman which belongs to Crocodilian order, closely related to the alligator. The largest of the Caiman species can grow to lengths of 5 meters and according to some reports even more than 6 meters in length! They apparently mostly eat fish, but the locals warn that they are not choosy when they are hungry. This sometimes includes their own young or the unfortunate human.

A Journey through Many Worlds

Joe makes a welcome cup of coffee, and one of the crew brings us a bowl of cooked nuts. Even though it is very late, I do not feel very tired, and while I peer into the dark jungle, I start to feel excited at the prospect of getting underway on the Jurua River at last—something that is drawing closer and closer all the while.

It is Sunday on the Ucayali. According to the skipper, we will reach the mouth of the Sheshea by about 16h00. At a small settlement, a few passengers disembark, and at last, a bit of space on board is freed up as they take their trade ware with them. At about 19h00 we eventually reach the river mouth. It does not look like there are any huts there and the crew says there is a small Indian settlement a few kilometers further on.

+ + + + + +

Fatima is a settlement of about 20 huts. Transportes Rios maneuvers herself in the darkness to the river bank, and the gangway is put out for us while the crew and captain help us carry our luggage off the boat. As we pass the huts, I again hear the loud sounds of the 80's pop song "Big in Japan" by Alphaville, set against the humming of a generator in the background. A large sign over the hut announces that it is the "Bodega Santa Fe"—the "Tavern of Holy Faith."

The inside of the hut has a slightly unholy appearance of a squatter camps pub, with Indians and half Indians talking and screaming away noisily and enthusiastically. Julio is the owner and easily the drunkest person present. He stands behind a rough wooden counter and behind him are his tools of the trade: rows of bottles and a few tins of fish and beef.

"Amigos!" he greets us, beer in hand while tempting the earth's gravitational field as if attempting to stand on a rubber duck in a slightly turbulent wind. He even talks a few words of English and explains to us that we are absolutely most welcome to stay overnight if we wish.

As a matter of fact, we can stay forever should it be our desire. There is a place for us to lock up our equipment and we can put up our hammocks on the huts outside deck. After

Up the Ucayali

we have declined his offer of beer no less than four times, he forgets about us and leave us alone to get a good night's rest next to the Yamaha generator.

A Macaw kindly announces the arrival of a new day by playing the harp on Joe's hammock ropes. At 08h00 Julio greets us once again, with yet another fresh beer in his hand. Big in Japan must be his favorite song, or maybe his only song for it is playing once again. I gather up my fishing tackle and stroll down to the river to practice my newly found skill while Joe goes off to explore the village with his camera. Without much effort, I catch two large barbers. Fishing is easy, I decide, I can't see what the big fuss is all about.

Joe prepares the fish, along with spaghetti and the inevitable barbecued bananas. It is our first proper meal in a few days, and the fish taste particularly good. I had always heard that river fish tasted like mud, but that was obviously just a rumor spread by city slickers. But I cannot help thinking maybe it does not taste so bad because we are already hungry? I shut the thought out of my mind.

It is after lunch that Julio offers me a beer again—an offer I now take up. It is sweltering, and the ice cold beer called 'Juan' he has given me tastes just fine. Julio has been hitting the bottle since early in the morning, and his short round wife wanders around, barking a few words in his direction every now and then. While I drink my second beer, Julio decides that we are the best friends ever, and gives me an ocelot skin as a present. I explain to him that I will not be able to take it, but he insists.

The ocelot looks almost like a small Jaguar and lives on smaller mammals, birds, fish, and reptiles. The animal's beautiful fur with its dark spots and stripes is one of the reasons it is endangered. In the interim, Joe calls me to come and help prepare some food. As we are busy, Julio approaches and offers to take us up the River for 200 soles. The price is outrageous, and in any event, Julio is permanently drunk, and we thus turn down his offer. Julio takes this refusal very personally, and as if he cannot believe it, he gets very aggressive all of a sudden.

69

A Journey through Many Worlds

"Then you pay 50 soles a night to stay here!" he shouts at us. It looks like he wants to subsidize his alcoholic costs at our expense. We decide to pack up and look for somewhere else to stay. Even though it is already dark, we decide it might be safer to put up our tent somewhere rather than deliver ourselves into the hands of a drunken opportunist.

"No, you stay here!", Julio says while we pack up. "We go, Julio, and here is the skin you gave me before you want me to pay for it too!", I reply.

"No, take it, please! You my friend!" The man is clearly confused, and I begin to get the idea that his short round wife is behind his dramatic mood swing. Two huts further down along the dirt road, we are offered a sleeping place. It is a small wooden room in one of the huts, and the quiet owner tells us that we do not need to pay him anything. He points in the direction of the Bodega and says "Julio loco"—Julio is crazy. Then we are offered supper: "Sopa de loricaria."

Once again, we are given particularly delicious fish which our host has cooked in water. These loricarias are about 30 cm long and although covered on the outside with hard armor "plates," the meat underneath is very favorable and soft.

We spend a quiet evening without a generator to keep us company and wake up the next morning feeling refreshed. Joe chats to one of the locals, Antonio, who promises to take us up the Sheshea River at a very good price. He has his own canoe and can take us first thing the next morning. Antonio promises to confirm with us no later than 17h00, for the arrangements of the following day.

By nightfall, however, there is still no sign of Antonio. While Joe starts up the stove to cook some vegetables outside the hut, I stroll down the long dirt road in the direction where Antonio said his hut was located. At places alongside the path, there are Indian huts.

The further away from the generator one goes, the more primitive the huts become. Later the path becomes smaller, and the huts get fewer and fewer. Here and there groups of

70

Up the Ucayali

Indians sit around fires and sing monotonous songs. It is a strange experience—almost like walking back in time, and even though I cannot see properly in front of me, something stops me from switching on my flashlight.

I felt guilty and uneasy, an intruder from the future into the past. I want to melt into the shadows and move away silently. Even though the Indians ignore me, they are aware that I am there. I can feel it... At a bunch of banana trees, a track leads off in the direction of the river. The trees get thicker, and the darkness becomes palpable. I finally switch on my flashlight and start walking faster. Antonio must now be close.

The night sounds are almost hypnotic, and for the first time I feel vulnerable, I am being watched, I know it for sure. I spin round as I hear a branch break behind me. A little way down the path I look into two glowing eyes staring at me, motionless. The Jaguar is king of the Amazon jungle. This powerful animal moves and hunts mostly at night, and when fully grown is almost two meters long. For countless generations the Indians have known him as "Yaguar"— he who kills with a leap—and with a body weight of 135 kilograms, double my own, I don't really want him on my back. Nor on my chest, come to think of it. I freeze on the spot. This is not because I know this is, in fact, the best thing to do, but simply because my legs will not move.

After what seems like a lifetime, the animal breaks its stare and turns away. By the Petzl's light, I see a profile of a thin dog which is now slowly walking back along the path. I realize that I am breathing again.

My mission is unsuccessful: I have not found Antonio. But after my encounter with the fearsome thin dog, I am also not really interested anymore, and I walk quickly back to where Joe is still struggling with the stove. "This is shit! I can't get the bloody stove to work properly!" Joe mutters in a frustrated voice, brushing away a sweated up lock of hair from his forehead.

"Did you find Antonio?" he asked. "No, I'll have a look in the morning" Early in the morning I see that the mist hangs

A Journey through Many Worlds

over the river in a thick blanket. The nights get cold, and I place our kettle on one of the Indian fires which have burned all night. I really enjoy a hot cup of coffee first thing in the morning.

But Antonio has vanished. One of the other locals tells Joe that the water level of the Sheshea is very low and that it is only possible to travel half way up the river with a canoe. The rest of the way will have to be tackled by foot. This will be madness for us with our more than 100 kilograms of equipment.

Further complicating matters is the fact that there are no roads in this area. The rivers serve as transport paths between the towns and villages, and in the dry season, many places are isolated from the outside world for months at a time. Our best bet seems to be to take our chances and go up further with the Ucayali to a town with the curious name of Nuevo Italia—'New Italy.'

Although it is not indicated on any of our maps, the locals assure us that a new logging route has been established running from Nuevo Italia to the Brazilian border. This is a chance we will have to take, and I hope that we can somehow get transport along the way.

We spent the afternoon taking pictures of Iguanas. The green, striped reptile is everywhere but is a careful creature. For many Indians, the Iguanas are a delicacy, but here in Fatima at least it seems the locals do not share this opinion. With a length of up to two meters, they look like miniature dinosaurs, sporting a row of erect armor points down their backs to their tails. All four feet end in five slim toes with long sharp nails used to climb trees. Although they appear on sight to be dangerous, the adult reptiles are herbivorous, while the young ones eat insects.

A batalon arrives just after midday, and we hurriedly load our baggage on board. The skipper says it will take about 5 hours to reach Nuevo Italia.

Along the way, we stop at several settlements to offload people and supplies. At one such village, a group of wooden

72

Up the Ucayali

structures, covered with palm leaves, sport large pieces of white fish drying in the sun. The boat offloads about 20 bags of 50-kilogram salt clearly marked "Industrial salt—not for human consumption." One of the passengers explains that it is used to salt the fish before being dried.

The dried fish is the favorite and tasty pirarucu; also know as arapaima or paiche. It is one of the largest fresh water fish found anywhere, with the largest being recorded at over four meters and 250 kilograms! The scales of the pirarucu are as large as a small palm tree, and the Indians have used the scales as a nail file for centuries.

As a result of the fish's size, it is caught with a harpoon, even though visibility in the muddy water is limited to a few centimeters at most. The Indians have devised a cunning plan to catch the fish: they put sticks into the water to mark out the current flow.

When a pirarucu swims past, the stick's movement indicates its presence. The patient fisherman then throws his harpoon into the brown water, at just the right place which experience has taught him.

The only trouble is that as the population has increased, the fish have become scarcer—and smaller.

Chapter 9
Meeting Marco Polo and Friends—
Good Men Doing Bad Things

"The only thing necessary for the triumph of evil is for good men to do nothing."

—Edmund Burke

When we finally reach Nuevo Italia, I wait with our baggage on the river bank while Joe sets off in search of accommodation. The town is much more modern and bigger than Fatima. The reason is apparent: Nuevo Italia is a logging base.

Trucks, earth moving equipment, and people armed with modern chain saws move out from this base into the rain forest in search of precious woods such as mahogany. First, they cut a road into the forest and then at 90-degree angles they cut open branch roads from this main arterial route. Alongside these side roads, they then seek out trees to be cut down.

On satellite pictures, the resulting devastation looks like a fishbone trail of destruction. The problem is that it is not only the mahogany trees which are damaged - for each and every tree that is cut down, a further 28 trees are damaged on average. The fine balance of the ecosystem is thus disturbed, and the entire chain—jungle, plants, and animals—suffer as a result.

Something else these people do not realize—or maybe they do, and they just ignore it—is that humans are ultimately going to suffer as well. These roads opened up will be used by settlers to reach previously unreachable places in the rainforest, thereby further diminishing its size.

Meeting Marco Polo

"Let's go, I found a place to stay, Johan," Joe calls. Our baggage now consists of a mere nine items, including camera bags, backpacks, suitcases, etc. With great difficulty, we carry it all up against the steep river bank to a nearby house. The friendly owners thereof operate a small shop from their backyard, and a tall wooden fence rings the property.

For ten soles per day, I suppose we could not exactly expect the Ritz, and the small wooden room which we get is just big enough for a single bed and small table.

I decide to erect the tent outside, leaving Joe to share the space with the baggage. The bathroom is an even smaller wooden building in the back yard. Water comes from a pit alongside the 'bathroom.' You can pour some into a large bin in which you can wash.

All the while, legions of mosquitoes descend on one, and it becomes a struggle to clean before being sucked dry by the vampire like swarms. As Joe struggles once again to get the stove to work, the woman of the house takes pity on him and allows us to use the gas stove in the kitchen.

Senhor Jerry Rios, the local municipal authority, is a man who makes himself extremely scarce, or so it seems. We set off in search of him this morning we are in search of him because we really need an "exit" stamp from Peru in our passports.

If all goes according to plan, we will shortly be in Brazil, and if we arrive there without an exit stamp from Peru, trouble is our most likely outcome. Also, we would like to get hold of proper maps of the area, as ours are quite vague recently.

A young Indian offers to take us to find senhor Rios. We walk through many thick bush areas, over tree stumps, river streams, past old broken down huts and eventually end, out of breath and more than an hour later, exactly where we started. But at least Jerry Rios is here, waiting for us.

He explains to Joe that there are no maps of which he is aware, and I can see from his expression that he apparently thinks we are crazy to even ask for such a thing. Furthermore,

75

A Journey through Many Worlds

he says, we have to get our exit stamps from "Tenente Santiago"—Lieutenant Santiago. As far as transport to the border, there is only one man who can help us: Senhor Coco. Senhor Coco is in control of the logging route up to the border. He stays on the riverbank, close to where we have taken up accommodation.

We meet Senhor Coco in the bar next to his house, and after listening with great patience to our story, he says there will be no problem as long as we only move along the logging route. Recent rain has flooded many of the roads, he adds, and the next set of trucks will only leave in a few day's time, once things have dried out a bit. In the meantime, we must just wait patiently.

Ok, then I guess it's time to improve my new survival sport—fishing, I think. For this purpose, I have acquired a professional instructor. Ricardo, or Ricci for short, is the nine-year-old son of the shop owner. He accompanies me to the riverside where I attempt to catch fresh lunch for Joe and myself.

The bait is a small piece of chicken which Ricci has cunningly stolen from his mother's kitchen for this purpose. Within seconds of the hook landing in the water, the line pulls stiff with a jerk and then goes limp almost as fast. I no longer feel the weight of the bait, and begin reeling the six-meter line back in. Nothing remains of the hook or bait.

"Por que?", I ask Ricci. "Ah, Piranha," he answers as a matter of fact. Amazon fishing lesson number one: use a piece of wire or cable between the hook and the line, because piranhas have very sharp teeth . . .

I think back to the 1914 book by American president Theodore Roosevelt, 'Through the Brazilian Wilderness' in which he wrote that piranhas "are the most ferocious fish in the world." Roosevelt tells the story of a man who was attacked by these small but dangerous fish.

According to the story, all that remained of the poor man was his skeleton. Now, in principle, I generally disbelieve anything that a politician has to say, but what is a fact is that

76

Meeting Marco Polo

piranhas have a well-known reputation for aggressiveness and they are indeed bloodthirsty.

What few people know, however, is that most of the diet of 30+ species (some people claim there are up to 60 species!) of piranha is in fact vegetarian. Those piranhas trapped in pools or lakes are at their most dangerous in the dry season when their food supply has dwindled. (Come to think of it— it is now the "dry" season here...)

The most well known of the piranha species is the red-bellied piranha (Pygocentrus Nattereri), Pana Roja, and it is also known as being one of the world's most dangerous fresh water fish. Generally, they grow around 14–26 cm in length (5.5–10.2 in).

I tie a piece of wire, about five centimeters long, between a new hook and the fishing line, and try again. The piranha takes the bait almost immediately, and I feel a burning sensation as the line cuts my right-hand index finger.

I pull on the line, walking backward while Ricci shouts fast and unfamiliar instructions in excited Spanish. The shiny, jumping piranha is about 40cm long and surprisingly strong for his size. "Aaah! Muy Grande piranha!", shouts Ricci in a high pitch voice.

He shakes my hand as if I have won first prize in an international fishing competition. I deliver the coup de grâce to the fish with a piece of wood and take the hook out of its mouth with my Leatherman. The teeth are small in comparison to his body, about 6-7 millimeters, but they are as sharp as razor blades.

Three hours later, Ricci and I return with five piranhas hanging from a stick. This is obviously much too much food for Joe and myself, so I decide to give the big piranha to Ricci as he was so friendly and helpful.

"Tank you, Juan," he says in broken English and runs away to show his parents. We barbecue the other piranhas and eat them with chips that Joe has prepared. Although they are very bony, they are nice. Eat or be eaten is the law here, I guess!

A Journey through Many Worlds

Around 19h00, we knock on Tenente Santiago's door. One of many children in the house opens the door. Santiago is at his dinner table with his wife and those children for whom there is place at the table. Joe apologizes and says we will come back later. "No problema," Santiago assures us. He is a thin, friendly man and listens to Joe's request apon which he begins to look for his stamp excitedly.

The area where he concentrates his search is a small table piled full of other items. It seems as if he does not use this stamp very often. Eventually he finds the stamp—under a Garfield wall clock with no batteries.

He stamps the passports and then with great self-importance, writes his name and the date underneath in blue pen—4 August 2002. Now we can legally leave this country! All we have to do is to get to the Brazilian border, about 120 kilometers away. How difficult can that be?

I hope that the ground will dry extra quickly. It is getting a bit boring around here, and we want to get to the river as fast as possible so that we can stop being reliant upon other people for transport.

Today, one of the locals, Fernando, came to talk with me while Joe took his afternoon nap. Fernando's dark eyes were unusually close together, and his white shirt looked as oily as his hair. "You go Brazil on Rio?", he asked in broken English. "Si!" I reply

"You can make money. I have a parcel that must go Brazil" , he states while observing around us.

"What kind of parcel is it?"

"Ah Senhor, you ask lot of questions. Well, it is 10 kg of a white powder, but you can make lots of money! Trust me!"

I realize that we were maybe not as fresh looking as when we started, but I didn't think we had already dropped down to looking like drug runners. Fernando had of course been watching us from the time we arrived, and when he heard we were going to enter Brazil through a place that did not have any border post, he realized this was the ideal manner

Meeting Marco Polo

in which to get his consignment delivered.

The other alternative was that our friend Fernando was an 'agent provocateur' working for the Peruvian police or the USA's Drug Enforcement Administration (DEA) and was trying to set a trap for us. "No thank you, Fernando. We cannot do it."

"You think about it senhor, lots money... lots.", he says with a sly and suppressed smile.

There is nothing to think about, apart from all the moral arguments one would have about smuggling 10 kilograms of cocaine, the real clincher in the discussion is that arrest for such an offense would mean a lifetime sentence eating moldy old potatoes in dim light in a stinking, rat infested Peruvian cell.

Late one evening, one of the truck drivers arrives to ask if we are the ones who are going to come with him. They are leaving now.

We quickly knock down the tent, pack hastily, and when we stagger into the road with our mountain of luggage, we're told that we actually cannot go with them after all. Our would-be driver explains that his immediate boss came to hear of the arrangement, and ordered him not to take us. It has something to do with the fact that we are photographers. Something tells me that this particular logging operation is not the legal type. We are now really quite pissed off.

Returning to our little wooden room, we consider the alternatives: if we cannot use the logging route, we will have to go back to Pucallpa and try and find an alternative route to the river. We slouch around in a depression for a day, and then, like manna from heaven, our salvation arrives: at a nearby truck shed there is a burst of activity, and we step over to meet a man named Javier.

He is a well built big man, who works for Coco and who is apparently in control of a group of trucks which are set to depart for the Tamaya logging camp in the morning.

The camp is located on the way to the Brazilian border. We

A Journey through Many Worlds

can come along, he says, but we cannot take any pictures. He has apparently had problems before with environmentalists.

These conditions are no problem—just as long as we can get away from here. To avoid a repetition of the previous evening's fiasco, we decide to sleep that night in the shed where all the trucks are kept.

With a "Vaya con Dios" (Go with God) and a worried expression on his face, our wooden room host bids us farewell, as Ricci performs in the background with tears in his eyes because he wants to come with us.

It is still dark when the trucks start up the next morning. Diesel fumes quickly put an end to our hours of leisure, and my throat soon burns from the smoke. Joe and I take up an uncomfortable position in the top of the fourth and last truck in convoy.

Our seats consist of blue drums of fuel. Fuel for all the chainsaws and vehicles which slash their way through the jungle, even now, as you read these words. The four trucks follow a yellow front end loader. Right from the very beginning, we see that this is going to be no easy ride. The road we are using is still very new, and the front end loader must help push one or more of the trucks out of the mud now and then. After a day of struggling, Javier decides that we must strike camp for the night.

I mark our position on the GPS: it has taken a whole day to travel exactly 75 kilometers from Nuevo Italia. One of the truck drivers gets a hunting rifle out of his car and walks in the direction of a small river about 200 meters from the road. I am still busy putting up our tent when I hear the shot. The tapir has in all likelihood never before even heard a rifle shot, much less having seen a human. He was just going for a drink in the cool water after a hot Amazon day. This brown, gray animal is related to the horse and has a lengthy, highly maneuverable snout with which he eats berries and fruit.

When the bullet hit the unsuspecting 200-kilogram animal in the right-hand flank, he collapses with a last warning shout. One less of a species that is already on the

Meeting Marco Polo

point of extinction.

The bloody carcass is dropped down in front of our tent, and Javier finds it amusing that we do not wish to share in this feast. Can we blame them? They cut down trees for a living; they do it to the best of their ability and are probably even proud of what they do. For them, the tapir is not an endangered species. They do not even know what an endangered species is. For them it is food: it is survival.

The real guilty parties are those people in the rest of the world who buy the wood and thereby create the market demand. Those civilized westerners know full well what endangered species are, do not know hunger, and they don't give a shit.

After a long night, we leave early the next morning. Many hours later, the thick forest vanishes, and we stop in a large clearing. Hundreds of fuel drums stand in rows under palm leaves which provide a little bit of protection against the merciless sun. Or is it to camouflage it from aerial observation? We are in Tamaya.

+ + + + + +

S 9° 30' 48.7" W 73°15' 35.5"

Camp Tamaya is named after a nearby river. Apart from the drums, a large hut, and a few vehicles, there is nothing else here. Once we have offloaded our baggage, Joe takes the opportunity to talk to Hernando, the camp commander. He is very reserved and agrees that we can stay at the camp for a while—temporarily.

As soon as vehicles leave in the direction of the Brazilian border, he will let us know. The days at Tamaya go by slowly, and I pass the time by catching fish and taking pictures of butterflies.

I build a shelter on the river sand as a protection against the sun and spend many hours there. One morning while on my way for an early morning fishing trip, I become aware of a strange noise emanating from the thick forest on the other side of the river.

A Journey through Many Worlds

The best way I can describe it sounded like the drone of an approaching storm. It gets louder and louder and then suddenly vanishes again. It is most strange, I think, there is no wind, and the trees and leaves are dead still.

I take off my boots and walk through the shallow, cold water of the Tamaya. Then the strange noise starts once again and stops just as suddenly. It's definitely not the sound of the wind, but what is it? It sounds so weird, almost supernatural. We will hear this strange sound many times shortly. High in the trees, almost out of sight, is a group of howler monkeys. They live in troops of up to 40 and get their name from their unique screams which can be heard up to three kilometers away.

They are most vociferous in the morning, or when there is danger around. With dinner in hand—a piranha and two catfish—I walk back to the camp. We cook the fish, remove the bones and flavor it with a bit of curry powder and onions. With a side serving of rice, it is most certainly one of our best meals to date.

"Hi, there!" We are not used to hearing English and look up in surprise. In front of us stands a man of about 25, shirtless and with a dirty pair of pants. "I am Marco Polo."

Yeah right! And I am Captain Cook, I think. Then I remember meeting a guy called Vasco da Gama when I was in the army in 1987, and decide to give Marco Polo the benefit of the doubt for now.

It's hard to associate the young man with these intelligent eyes with logging. He talks for a long time with Joe and I and asks many questions about our journey. He tells us that one day he wants to tour and see the world. Marco then tells Joe that he has heard that there was once a famous man with the same name as him and asks if we have ever heard of him. He listens with great pride and interest as Joe gives a shortened version of the famous Venetian merchant traveler.

That was the last time we ever saw Marco. I wonder if he will ever achieve his dream. Someone with intelligence and potential, condemned to chopping down trees for a living.

Meeting Marco Polo

The only life he knows. The next day a truck takes us to the next logging camp, Venado, a few kilometers further on. From here a truck leaves the next morning to the border, and Hernando has arranged for us to come along. I think he is delighted to be rid of us, and it is clear that very few of the loggers are happy when photographers are around. The atmosphere at Venado is, however, a lot more jovial, and a short Indian named Juan welcomes us warmly. He introduces us to Jorge, a solidly built man of around 40 with a neat shirt. He speaks broken but understandable English and tells us proudly that his mother was an Indian.

Our sleeping quarters for the night is pointed out to us: a palm covered shelter. The 'beds' are cut out of palm tree trunks, raised on poles. As the sun sets, Juan starts a big fire in front of the hut, and we prepare coffee for our host. It is a beautiful evening, and suddenly I realize that there are no mosquitoes around. By this time at Tamaya, the engorged insects would be staggering around, drunk on their bloody feast. I notice however that all the beds are each equipped with a mosquito net, and I ask Juan for an explanation.

"Muchos mosquitos aqui?", I ask.

"No no, senhor, no mosquito! Musquitos Nada problemo", Juan replies while shaking his head. I noticed a puzzled look on his face. Now I am curious. Then I point out the mosquito nets hanging over the beds.

"Ahh, no mosquito! Senhor...muchos Vampiro!"

Joe assures me I have heard correctly. The nets are not for mosquitoes, but for "Vampiro."

I am aghast: this is no Hollywood creation, they really do exist here! There are three species and all of them native to Central and South America.

They are small bats, and they live in colonies of up to a thousand. They go to work quite scientifically: with heat sensors they detect a blood rich area on their prey, and hover over the selected area, flapping their wings which produce some kind of anesthetic effect. Then they cut small holes with their teeth in the sleeping prey's skin and lick up the

A Journey through Many Worlds

blood, simultaneously allowing an enzyme in its saliva to mix with the blood, preventing it from clotting.

Before the advent of the luxury of a mosquito net, the Indians used to sleep with their feet towards a fire, and cover their heads with leaves or cloth. Fortunately, we wake up in the morning with the same quantity of blood as when we went to sleep. Alongside our designated sleeping place an old Dodge truck is parked, and Juan tells us to get ready to leave.

Chapter 10
The Long Road to Sawawo

"Exploring is delightful to look forward to and back upon, but it is not comfortable at the time unless it be of such an easy nature as not to deserve the name."

—Samuel Butler

Late August 2002. We started loading our equipment and baggage onto the already overloaded blood red Dodge truck. We know that this is our last chance, for a long time, to get to Sawawo. Only a few days before, Joe and I did not even know that this tiny Indian town existed, but now we know all too well that it lies on the border between Peru and Brazil, and, more importantly, near a river that will bring us to the Jurua. At least, this is what we hope.

The road that we are now following was only completed a few months previously. 'Road' would be an overstatement—a better description would be a mud track which winds its way through virgin rainforest and does not appear on any map. Joe adjusts his straw hat on his head, and we are ready to leave, while our driver, a thin Fidel Castro look-alike, orders a further two diesel drums to be loaded on to the already creaking truck.

Sounding like a dying wind pump, the Dodge groans its way out of the camp. Our worst fears are realized when a miserable 200 meters further, the truck comes to a complete stop in the deep red brown mud. Castro screams orders in some unintelligible dialect of a language that we presume to be Spanish. Some of the newly embarked passengers climb off again and begin chopping down branches and leaves

A Journey through Many Worlds

from the surrounding bush with their machetes. These are thrown over the mud and jammed in under the wheels. Our hearts sink when all this to no avail and the Dodge's wheels merely spin themselves deeper into the mud.

Seemingly at ease, Castro climbs out on the track and begins walking back towards the camp. Some of the other passengers follow, while others get out and calmly sit alongside the road in the shadow of the trees. "Joe, what's happening?" I say anxiously. "I don't know—they spoke of another truck."

'Oh, shit...'

A mere three hours later, Castro comes walking back, sporting something that looks like a piece of pawpaw stuck on his cheek. Once again he orders his passengers to start chopping up branches and leaves and putting them under the wheels.

This time, however, it looks like they really want to get the truck out and I wonder if the three-hour delay was merely a tactic on Castro's part to make them more enthusiastic about the job. In any event, the increased vigor of the activity ensures that the Dodge pulls itself out of the mud, and it looks like we are finally on our way!

Our enthusiasm is soon dampened by the baking sun that burns its way through our thin shirts and hats. I feel as if mine is made of rice paper. We grind along for a further five kilometers before, to our horror, we slide to a halt once again. This time the truck faces a steep rise and its smooth tires simply get no grip on the flat dry mud. We have a sense of déjà vu as Castro tries half-heartedly to coax the track up the hill. His now once again disembarked passengers stand idly around, most looking as if they are waiting for a miracle. They look at each other and calmly begin chatting as if this is an everyday occurrence. I am nearly overcome by frustration, desperation, and helplessness. The insects attack even if you stand still for a minute. The worst sort is a small fly type bug with a vicious bite, the locals call it a 'pumi', and we called them bastards.

The Long Road to Sawawo

"Joe, I've had it with this shit, I'm walking," I grunt. "OK," says Joe, apparently too disgusted with the state of the truck to argue. Looking back on it, and I find it difficult to believe that the frustration was so overpowering that I could have even considered doing such a stupid thing.

But, walk I did, all alone and without any water (our water was in any event already finished by then). Carrying only my camera bag and my trusted Leatherman, I set off down the jungle path, trying to forget about my frustration. The sun, jungle, and insects plague me all the way, and I wondered how Indiana Jones managed to look so fresh at his destination.

It was now 14h00, and with the last tiny bit of mental clarity which I still had, I calculated that I had another 3 hours walk to the next logging camp called Camp 20—presuming of course, that Castro's distances were correct. The first few hours walk felt unbelievable—I was alone on a ground road in the heart of the Amazon, on a road which had never been walked by any tourist ever before.

Odors from the thick bushes and trees on either side of the path wafted down, smells that will always be with me. Apes shrieked warnings to each other high in the trees, and the din of smaller insects seemed to emanate from everywhere. By the late afternoon, I realized with a shock that I have to find water—urgently.

My mouth and lips are cracked from the heat, and I feel my pace slowing with each step. In my semi-delirium I now find another obstacle—the road has come to a fork. I stand and ponder my choice: if I choose the wrong road, I will miss Camp 20 and Joe will probably have an interesting story to relate to my surviving family back home.

In desperation, I sit down in the middle of the road—at least the chances of being run over are slim. Johan, I think to myself, you are the single greatest fucking idiot in South America. No food, water, flashlight, or matches. Would it not have been a better idea to wait with the Dodge? A few clouds soften the sharp light of the moon. The darkness is now overpowering, and the jungle has stopped being a place

A Journey through Many Worlds

of fascination and instead looks uninviting. The noises from the dense trees have now become threatening, and I feel that I dare not sit still. I do a quick calculation: if the Dodge is still in the same place, I will have to walk about 30 kilometers all the way back.

I check my watch—it is now 21h00 I feel like I'm going to drop, so I speed up the process by laying down flat on the road. All I want to do is rest a while. As I close my eyes, I hear a droning noise. Is this what it feels like to die I ask myself. I have read stories of people who have had "near death" experiences and am now waiting for that bright light they talk about.

But the bright light which shines in my eyes turns out to be that of a Honda motorcycle. I leap up and manage to stop the astounded motorcyclist. In my breathless and tattered Spanish, I ask him where he is going. "Sawawo," is his answer, his face belying his disbelief at finding me lying in the road in the middle of the jungle. I don't care. Hallelujah!

With sore hips and legs, I jump on the back of the motorcycle, and we are off. The ride to Camp 20 seems to take an eternity. Every now and then I must jump off the motorbike so that it can slip and slide its way up the muddy hills.

At one stage a huge tapir appears in the motorcycle's headlight, a few meters in front of us. The driver takes fright and nearly loses control as the blinded animal rushers wildly back into the bush. The only light in Camp 20 comes from a tiny oil lamp, which exudes a glow only slightly stronger than a starved glow worm.

Everyone is already asleep after a hard day's work destroying the jungle. Outside the camp, I see rows of huge mahogany trees, cut down and laid down like massacred corpses, and a little further along, rows of diesel and petrol drums.

A fat woman, reeking of sleep, stumbles out from underneath one of the palm-covered structures. Two men follow her. I have heard strange stories about these loggers,

The Long Road to Sawawo

and doubtless, they have heard strange stories about photographers, especially those with white faces who do not speak the local language. I am not at ease.

"Agua por favor!!!' I start, but they just laugh at my Spanish. Now I am sure that my last moment has come. I probably look like it anyway. But my guardian angel is with me. The fat woman offers me coffee. No! Water, please, now!

My tongue is swollen in my mouth, and my voice sounds strange. Water, plain pure water, tastes like the nectar of the gods. I'm given fresh fish, barbecued on open coals. Followed by the coffee, which puts in a reappearance, in red plastic bowls, similar to those that I use at home to feed my cat. The granules—at least that as I think and hope they are—float around in the coffee, but I tell you what, it tastes fantastic.

It is late in the evening by the time I get shown a place to sleep. It is under one of the palm-covered structures—right alongside the fat woman. Even though I am tired, tired beyond words, the fat woman keeps me awake by snoring like an electric chainsaw, easily drowning the wildest chirruping of the jungle animals.

These loggers take work seriously. My bed consists of a sheet which I fold around myself as I lie on the floor. My jeans serve as a pillow, and I cling to my camera bag as a dying man clings to life. At half past three, I notice that the snorer's drone has changed of tone. I listen carefully—I realize that I can, in fact, hear the hum of a truck. The Dodge is nearly here!

Suddenly the camp comes alive once again. The fire resurrected and new coffee brewed. From between the banana trees, a child appears with the dirty pot full of meat of dubious origin. Fortunately, it is still dark, and I'm starving. I suppress my sense of smell—I need the food!

After what seems to be an exotic meal of meat and cooked bananas, I realize that the far off hum of the truck has stopped. This does not appear to bother anyone else in the camp. I wait anxiously, but by 06h00 I have given up hope, and I leave once again with my trusty motorcyclist friend.

A Journey through Many Worlds

The Dodge has perhaps taken the other road, and I do not want to take the chance of waiting here if they are never going to come this way.

Camp 20 doesn't qualify as my idea of a retirement village, especially after that night without earmuffs and a mosquito net. The following 20 plus kilometers to Sawawo are not boring. It takes about an hour. Thorn bushes leap out at us from the side of the road as if they have a life of their own, and the blood flows freely down our arms and legs. The motorcyclist seems to be used to this, and although I am in pain, he never flinches, pausing only to cast me a pitiful look every now and then.

Parts of the road are still soaking from the recent rain, and we slide around like drunkards in a dodgem car. A group of five Scarlet Macaws screams at us from the air as they fly northwards. For a moment I see a bright yellow poison arrow frog as he bravely tries to cross the mud path.

Then I notice that the thick bush is becoming thinner and here and there, I see patches of complete aridification. Sawawo cannot be very far. The first huts appear on the right-hand side of the road, similar to what we have seen on the Ucayali, but more primitive.

Then we are in Sawawo.

Indian huts, children, dogs, and women with big eyes. Faces with eastern traits, painted in red dye drawn from seeds of local plants. The village lies on the border with Brazil and the banks of the Amonea River, a tributary of the Jurua. We have made it!

Or at the very least I have. Joe will follow shortly, I think to myself. My motorcyclist friend, who I have since discovered is named Ricardo, mumbles something unintelligible and leaves me.

"Sawawo aqui??"—Is this Sawawo? , I ask of the crowd of red faces now gathered around me. They burst out laughing, and I take this amusement as an affirmative answer, hoping that they find my ignorance funny and nothing else. I decided that I urgently need a cigarette.

90

The Long Road to Sawawo

"Onde loje??"—Where is a shop—I try to amuse the crowd further. I succeed—the gales of laughter make me blush, and I decide that I am not suited to the role of village clown. Can things get worse?

I am all alone, the lonely comedian, with a non-paying audience. It is not as if the Indians are unfriendly; it is just that I am now thoroughly sick and tired of everything. More out of desperation than anything else, I go and sit in front of one of the huts, hoping my audience will tire of my inactivity and disperse.

The sound of running water directly next to me snaps my consciousness back to normality. On the roof of the hut, an Indian boy, about six years old, dressed only in beads, urinates. It is not as if he cannot see me, on the contrary, he seems to want to see how close he can pee to me. His face is emotionless. I saw, I came, I got pissed upon. Thanks a lot, glad to see I am welcome.

A girl emerges from the hut alongside and begins to talk to me. Even though I don't understand anything, her tone of voice convinces me that I have nothing to fear. She gives me a few bananas and a cup of a strange sweet liquid in it. This is, I think to myself, a better manner in which to welcome a visitor. I realize it does not help to tell these people that you cannot speak their language. It only serves to spur them on to talk even faster.

I notice that the hut's floor is made of palm bark and stands about 1,5 meters above the ground, mounted on wooden poles. To get into the hut, you have to climb a piece of a tree stump in which three grooves have been cut. The raised floor offers a measure of protection against wild animals and snakes.

Furthermore, it is cooler because of the airflow underneath. The hut has no walls and supports a roof made of interwoven palm fronds. It is quite incredible how waterproof it is. Even in the most severe storms I never saw one leak.

However, the lack of walls is a serious problem during such a storm. Inside the hut, there are a couple of hammocks tied

A Journey through Many Worlds

to poles, which serve as beds. They offer me one. I accept. I hang my camera bag on one of the roof struts and lie down. There is, I decide, nothing better on earth than this new bed. I lie there and close my eyes. Ah, peace.

A sharp pain in my foot reminds me that I am not on the beach at Rio de Janeiro. The culprit is a black fly—at first sight, it appears to be a miniature version of a Buccaneer bomber. Later on, I will realize that it is just one of Sawawo's many pests.

During the day, you are dive bombed by biting flies, sand flies, and mosquitoes. At night an entirely new range of blood sucking monsters emerge and drive the mosquitoes away with their ferociousness, sending out their scouts in search of new victims like clockwork at 18h00 each night, retreating for the daytime bombing campaigns at 06h00. I wonder if they have an atomic clock, as you can tell the time by their prompt appearance and disappearance.

It is now late midday, and there is still no sign of Joe. I hope nothing has happened to him. A group of men appears from the bush, muscled and sweating, each armed with an orange and white Stihl chainsaw. They watch me with empty disinterested eyes. I suppose that is better than laughing at me; I console myself.

One of the men comes into my hut. "Joao," he introduces himself with an outstretched hand. His dark eyes seem to be honest, but this is put off slightly by the fact that he wears a necklace made of crocodile teeth. He starts to talk to me as he sits on the floor and takes off his shoes. There are no chairs or other furniture in the hut.

The roof struts serve as a storage place for clothes and food. Shiny pots hang here and there. Joao displays a lot more judgment than the rest of his village and appears to realize that I do not understand anything and can talk even less. He makes an effort to make himself understood.

Opening a right angled mosquito net, he lays down a blanket and indicates to me that this is where I must sleep. I thank him profusely—without a mosquito net, a person will

The Long Road to Sawawo

inevitably be sucked dry in an hour. The insect repellent I brought with me from South Africa has only limited success—in fact, it seems as if the mosquitoes regard it as more of a challenge rather than a deterrent.

As time goes on, other nets are set up in the hut, and I realize that some eight people sleep here.

Outside, bananas in oil are barbecued—dinner! I only realize how tired I am when I lay down on my blanket. Within seconds, I collapse into a deep sleep. I wake up with a fright—it is already light.

The drone of chainsaws heralds the start of a new working day. The mosquito nets have all disappeared, and the hammocks are once again in place.

In the middle of the village, there is a large open area, in which some children play. A bleached Peruvian flag flutter on a decidedly skew bamboo pole. Next to one of the huts stands a giant satellite dish, a foretaste of what awaits this once traditional village!

I think of the equipment on the Dodge, wherever it may be: a generator, corrugated iron sheets, cement, electrical equipment . . . an isolated Indian village is methodically being converted into a logging center.

The day passes slowly. By 14h00 I notice that something is happening. Women and children start gathering on the other side of the fields. Someone—or something—is coming! I recognize Juan and George, who I last saw on the Dodge. Now they are on foot, each carrying a bag.

With them are some other passengers from the Dodge, but alas, Joe is not amongst them. George explains in his broken English: "Your friend is OK. Dodge is fucked up. We walk. Your friend rest in Camp 20. He come tomorrow."

He adds that they called for help by radio and that a Volvo is on its way. Tomorrow, he says, the cargo will be transferred over to the Volvo and brought to Sawawo. At least I now know what is happening. The rest of the day is taken up with walking around, eating bananas, and talking to George.

A Journey through Many Worlds

The Indians weave a type of cotton that grows freely here. It is colored with Mahogany tree bark. Juan shows different types of plants to me, and George acts as interpreter. Apart from a variety of bananas, many other fruits grow here, including pawpaws, coconuts and so on.

The Cocona is an exotic fruit. Round shaped and reddish in color, it has a strange taste that reminds me slightly of tomato, but only somewhat more sour. Each fruit has between 800 to 2000 seeds, with a smooth, stiff skin covered in fine hairs. It is eaten as it is picked or pressed out into water to make an excellent drink that quenches the wildest thirst. Only later do I discover that the juice is also used as a treatment for head lice. . . Yuka (Manioc) grows all around here and makes up a large part of the basic diet.

There are many variants of this root plant, and it is served in many guises. It can be dangerous for the uninformed, as certain types are highly poisonous and must be prepared in a special way before it can be eaten. I shudder to think how they discovered which ones were poisonous and which were not. Unsurprisingly, Yuka is also the source of an alcoholic drink.

Farinha, or their version of maize, is sprinkled over other food sorts. This can be a little hard on the teeth but is tasty. The Indians have superstitions about the plant, and it is used as a medicine. A Cashew tree stands near to the river, its fruit not yet ripe. On each fruit or cashew apple, hangs a single nut. No wonder cashew nuts are so expensive.

It might sound as if Sawawo is the land of milk and honey. If only that were true! The above-mentioned fruit and foods do grow there, but as my luck would have it, nothing was ripe or available while we were there. We were confined to a diet consisting mainly of green bananas and Yuka –and believe me, you can get pretty tired of that fare very quickly.

The Indians have a peculiar eating pattern. Every day it consists of a watery Yuka porridge with bananas or cooked Yuka. Every now and then they will go and catch a wild pig—a Wangana—and even more rarely, will they catch a fish. My impression was that it was simply too much effort to catch

The Long Road to Sawawo

a pig or a fish, even though when they hunt, they use a 410 shotgun!

Fish, when they are caught, are shot with bows and arrows as often as they are caught with a line! Once they have exerted themselves to catch something, they overeat for a day or two and then revert to the Yuka and banana diet after that. You can see evidence of malnutrition amongst some of the children, especially the younger ones.

Items such as coffee, oil, sugar and so on, are brought in from Thaumaturgo in Brazil, by canoe—when the water level of the Amonea makes it possible. There is also a footpath to Breu where supplies can also be obtained. I am told it is a day or two's walk . . . The next day chaos erupts in the village.

Children run up to me and babble incessantly, waving in the direction of the road. I recognize the words "Gringo" and "shapeo"—'white man' and 'hat' . . . That can only be Joe! Sure enough, stumbling through the vegetation an exhausted looking Joe is appearing. His face looks thin and drawn, and sweat pours from him like the fountains at Trevi in Rome. In his hands, he holds his camera bag and my film case. The Volvo?

He has not seen it and had no idea where the rest of our baggage is. He has walked the entire distance as well. Joe collapses into a hanging canvas bed and quenches his thirst. Slightly revived, he begins to tell me his story: After the Dodge refused to go any further and I had started walking, Castro and his men had battled for several hours to get the truck to move once again.

They succeeded, but only for a short while, before they once again got stuck in the mud. Digging their way out once more, the Dodge moved forward again, only coming to a final halt, when its engine finally departed this earth for a better life elsewhere.

Castro and his crew were faced with no alternative but to take what they could carry and walk. Joe did what only a good photographer would do: sleeping bags, mosquito nets, and other luxuries were abandoned, and only the camera

95

A Journey through Many Worlds

equipment was taken! I was grateful—there were 150 films in my film case alone! It is not easy terrain to cross, especially not at night.

He stayed over at Camp 20 and took another day to catch up with me in Sawawo. Our situation was thus as follows: we had reached our immediate destination. Camera equipment and films in perfect condition.

The rest of our gear—food, medical supplies, tent, mosquito nets, etc., etc. was now behind us, about 35 kilometers away in an abandoned Dodge truck in the middle of the Amazon rain forest. Losing our kit could mean the end of our expedition. Not good at all.

"No problem! Dodge fucked up. Volvo here tomorrow with cargo. You rest", Jorge tries to calm us. I had been told that this mysterious Volvo was due in today already . . . "No problem."

Two days later it was still "No problem"—and there was also still no Volvo or cargo.

Chapter 11
Down The River of Dreadful Turns

"Not all those who wander are lost."

—J.R.R. Tolkien

Yucca has stopped tasting exotic, and apart from the fact that we are now getting quite hungry, it is time that things speed up a bit. To each of our inquiries about our equipment, there is a new excuse. The most recent one is that they have confirmed by radio that the Volvo is at Camp 20, but as a result of the rain, it must wait there until the road is dry. I don't believe anything they say anymore and am tired of sitting and waiting. To add to our joy, we don't have any malaria pills with us—it is still on the truck! I have had the delight of experiencing malaria once before, and do not want to retake the chance.

Malaria is a deadly disease that is transmitted by the bite of an infected Anopheles mosquito. Typical symptoms include fever, vomiting and headaches. If not treated properly it can end up in a seizure, coma, and death. It was the cause of more than 120 000 deaths worldwide in 2002.

On Saturday I tell Joe that I will have to walk back and look for our kit. Joe is not feeling good, so he will stay at Sawawo. Besides, one of us will have to watch our camera equipment to ensure it does not end up in some small Indian hands. I am sure they are lying to us and that the Dodge is exactly where we left it, hopefully with baggage and all if we are lucky. If this is so, then at least I can get the essential items into a backpack and bring them back. Joe draws up a

A Journey through Many Worlds

list of what he wants. It is, in any event, better to walk than to sit and wait and listen to empty promises in an exotic language, I rationalize to myself. Jorge and the others think I am crazy—the Volvo is almost here, they say. Yes, yes.

Nourished by a hearty Sawawo breakfast consisting of a few barbecued bananas and weak coffee, I leave early on Saturday on my quest. During my previous march, my boots began giving problems, the inner soles have rotted away, and a row of sharp shoe nails make their presence felt into the sole of my left foot. Once again it is a job for my trusty Leatherman.

The first part of the route is the most difficult. My boots clump up with mud, meaning that I slide more than I walk. Every few meters I have to stop to scrape the mud off my boots, as leaving it on means carrying unnecessary—and growing—weight.

By 08h00 it is already boiling hot. I see lots of birds around and early in the morning they play a prominent part in the background chorus of animal sounds. The fat lady at Camp 20 seems very pleased to see me while chainsaws drone in the forest around us. She gives me cocona juice, for which I am very grateful as I have no container with me to carry water. The Volvo is, of course, nowhere to be seen at the Camp, and I am strangely not surprised. Your muscles get stiff if you are inactive for too long, so after only a few minutes rest, I once again set off. Not long after leaving Camp 20 my body informs my brain that it needs water again. Urgently. Now.

Howler monkeys again begin their eerie, ghostly sounds drifting through the green surroundings. I find this distracting, making it difficult to focus.

A small stream runs a few feet slowly under a makeshift "bridge" consisting of tree trunks tied together with rope. The water reflects an unhealthy greenish brown color, but my body says "Great! It's WATER!!!"

While I stare at the stream, my brain suddenly recognizes a well-camouflaged form half submerged in the water. The Anaconda must be at least 25 cm (10 in) thick, and I can

Down The River of Dreadful Turns

see only about 1 meter of its length with no head visible. I remember the famous explorer Percy Fawcett describing a 20-meter anaconda he came across many years earlier near the Rio Negro.

No, I am not that thirsty—time to move on—brain and body agree. By late afternoon I arrive sweaty and thirsty at the Dodge—exactly where it came to a halt with Joe and the crew. Not even the tire track of a Volvo in sight. Once again, I am not surprised. I lack the power to climb onto the truck. Instead, I sit down on the road, my body is sore, and my one boot sole has come loose with my foot now squishing around in its private mud bath.

I sit and contemplate the meaning of life for about a half hour, and then get up to climb up on the Dodge and take the essential items off. My backpack and tent, the latter of which I then set up in the middle of the road, as this is the only clearing to be found. What is now the most important is fire and water.

Back to basics, this was how cavemen started out. Fortunately, I find a small stream not too far away. The quality of the water seems to be better. After long observation, I carefully and slowly approach the water's edge. This time with my hunting knife at the ready. After I quench my thirst and cool myself down a bit, I set off in search of wood. That might sound like a sine qua non in the Amazon.

But it is not as simple as it sounds to find dry wood. After a long search, I gather a few suitable pieces, which must burn until the morning at least. Dry branches or leaves to get the fire going—that is even harder to find. In the process, I overheat my lighter and the flint shoots out of its socket. Shit! I am forced back onto plan B.

In my backpack; I have an American "fire tool." This consists of a magnesium block with a flint on the one side. What you do is cut off pieces of the magnesium block with a knife, and then light them by scraping the flint with your knife above it. This is guaranteed to set a fire within, oh, at least the first 50 attempts, if you are adept at it.

A Journey through Many Worlds

The problem, however, remains to get the wet leaves to burn. The humidity is so high, and because the forest is so thick, direct sunlight is not much aid. Hence everything under the top layer of the forest is pretty much wet. Humidity levels of 94 percent are not unusual here. Ok, so on to plan C. I return to the Dodge. Aha!! on the back I find a tin of oil, and in the cab is a September 1987 Spanish language edition of Reader's Digest. I set to work and tear a few pages out of the Readers' Digest, and throw a spot of oil on them. On top of that, I pack some thin branches and then the larger pieces of wood.

The 'fire tool' eventually does its job, and soon I have a roaring campfire. McGuyver is now really hungry. My food supplies have dwindled to the point where I have a choice between rice and rice. The former is more appealing to me, so I choose it, and have a lovely cup of rice for supper.

Now the next challenge: night falls, the mosquitoes start their attack, and I have to shelter inside the tent to finish my food. I leave my muddy boots outside and finish my luxury meal in peace.

To my great surprise, I find that I am quickly satiated, and am forced to leave a portion of the rice for breakfast. There are some strange nocturnal sounds in this part of the world. At one stage I hear the thunderous crash of a tree falling. All kinds of primates scream - here, there and everywhere. I try to shout back at them, but their reaction indicates amusement rather than fear.

The thought of me sitting here alone in the middle of the virgin rain forest is overwhelming. Both exciting and yes, scary too. I am alone—only me surrounded by the living forest, now dark and mysterious. But am I really alone?

Although my body is exhausted, my brain refuses to switch off. Just above my head—outside, against the tent skin—I hear something scratching. It doesn't sound as if it could be too big. But the scratching sound is just enough to keep me awake—and worried. I move away from the side of the tent—just in case some animal with big teeth decides to have a general 'see-what-is-in-there-type-bite.' The

100

Down The River of Dreadful Turns

scratching noise continues with increasing intensity, but I have no desire to poke my head out to see what the source is—especially not when the mosquitoes are waiting to attack as well. For God's sake, go to sleep Johan.

Suddenly the scratching sound turns into a sliding noise, this time from two places above my head. The scratching monster has called its friend. I can see there will be no sleep for Johan tonight. Face your demon. I switch on my flashlight and cautiously open the tent, Kershaw hunting knife at the ready...

A truly amazing sight awaits me. Surrounded by a Disney wonder world, thousands of yellowish eyes surround me. My boots and two bags I left outside the tent are covered in moths! Their eyes reflect in my Petzl flashlight in fantastic color. Most are small white moths, but there are many others as well, different forms and shapes. The tent itself is almost invisible under a mountain of moths. I have never seen anything like it ever before.

I cannot see anything which could be causing the scratching noises, and I presume that it was a frog or something trying feast on the moths sitting on the tent. After each "attack" attempt it slides back off because it can't get a grip on the tent! Considerably less fearful, I climb back into my sleeping bag inside the tent. Even though the days are sweltering, the night cools off so quickly that it gets chilly.

I have barely laid down once again when the frogs—I hope they are frogs—renew their assault on the tent. It seems like five frogs are simultaneously trying to beat their way through the nylon tent. News of this favorite restaurant spreads quickly amongst the Frog population. It must be the great revenge of the frogs. I consider my defense: I am not French.

Try to sleep. Johan. Then a shrill screaming noise and fast scuffle make me sit bolt upright. Something has caught one of the frogs. A snake?... or something worse? The prospect of joining the Amazon food chain looms large in my mind once again. I try to convince myself that this thin nylon tent offers a lot of protection. I nearly fall asleep comforted by this thought, only to be woken again by a new set of strangling

A Journey through Many Worlds

noises, some close by and some far away. I even hear what is almost certainly a human voice screaming...

I can't help but think about reports of the so called "uncontacted" Indian tribes of the Amazon... Really, I am not dressed, equipped or in the mood for a contact tonight. Piss off!

When I get up, it is still early dawn. I must sort out our kit on the Dodge and try to get a bit more rest after the last evening's carry-on. Tomorrow morning I will start the trip back to Joe.

Early in the morning, it is once again unbelievably hot. There is a myriad of insects and far too many of them for my liking. I am stung for the umpteenth time by a vicious strain of horsefly, but the only advantage is that I am getting used to the pain. Butterflies, sporting the most incredible range of colors flap continually around my head as if they are feasting on me. And of course, interspersed are what seems to be millions of flies.

To sit in the tent is to commit suicide—slowly. If only there were a way to escape the humidity, heat, and insects. I find a piece of shadow on the side of the road, and lay down, covered by my mosquito net. It grants some peace from the insects but does nothing to help the heat situation. As soon as you sit still for a second, all the insects in the Amazon descend upon you. The only solution is to keep moving.

I figure out that it will now be impossible to walk back to Sawawo today. It is already too late. The rest of the day is spent walking up and down the road, trying to ward off the insects.

Near the Dodge, I find a Cocona bush with one ripe fruit and make myself a juice extract. Further along the road I find some dryish wood and throw it onto the fire. The alleged Volvo is still nowhere to be seen. When it starts to cool down slightly, I start trying to retrieve the kit from the Dodge. The canvas over the truck is packed with butterflies who are upset at my intrusion.

After a long search, I finally find everything of ours, even

Down The River of Dreadful Turns

the luxuries such as toothbrushes and soap. I have had enough river sand in my mouth, thank you very much. I pack everything into my backpack, and hope like hell we will not have to walk back to get the rest of the stuff.

That night, I sleep substantially better. A kettle, a piece of booty from the Dodge, is over the fire. I eat the last of the rice and wash it down with a cup of coffee. Oh, how nice it is to have the luxuries once again. After I have put some more wood on the fire and driven the wild animals away with my version of an Andrea Bocelli medley, I feel more at ease. I even have confidence that in the morning, I will make short work of the trek back. I close my eyes, forget about food chains, and collapse into a deep sleep.

While the fire is still crackling, I awake with a fright. I fold up the tent, pack the last of the goods into my backpack and put on my boots, newly restored with masking tape. I fill my water bottle at the stream—it will be my only water until Camp 20.

The return journey takes its time. The stick I picked up to help get up the hills seems to help more than I anticipated. After about two hours of walking, I stop to rest. When I slide the backpack off, I feel that my back is ice cold. Bugs of all sorts hum around me as I drink some water and only minutes later pick up the cudgels and carry on. It does not help to rest for long; it only makes the muscles lazy.

I am walking merrily when I hear a drone of an engine. Is this the return of the motorbike? No, Johan, you are hallucinating, just carry on walking. The drone gets louder and louder, and I walk faster and faster. This process repeats itself several times, and I convince myself that it is a hallucination. Only when the ground starts vibrating, and I hear the noise right behind me, do I look back.

At the steering wheel of the White Volvo is none other than the incompetent Dodge driver, Castro. It is with great effort that I pass up my backpack to the willing hands on the vehicle.

My nearly lame legs just clamber up the tire, and I find

A Journey through Many Worlds

the space between all the baggage quite comfortable as I lay down between the packets of cement, planks, and six other people. I note that the Dodge's load has not been loaded over as promised, but I don't care that much any more.

The Volvo is, as I should have expected, unable to progress more than a few kilometers before it too is overwhelmed by the mud. Machetes are unpacked, palm branches are cut down and placed under the wheels.

A half hour later and we are once again on our way. We stop at Camp 20. Diesel drums are offloaded, and we drink water and eat papayas. About five kilometers from Sawawo the Volvo decides that it also needs a rest, and locked in dark red mud, it shudders to a halt.

The incompetent driver decides it is not even worth trying to dig the vehicle out, and so it must stay there until the ground is dry. Cursing, I carry on with my trek by foot. It is late afternoon when I start on the last climb to Sawawo. The standard welcoming party of red faced curious onlookers gathers. This time it is my large Karrimor backpack which seems to be the focal point of their interest.

"I've got a fever Johan," Joe says to me with a blanched face from his hammock. I immediately think of malaria. No, anything but that. From the medical box, I take two Larium tablets for myself and Joe. He tells me it is a long time since he last ate.

"I can't stand this food anymore. Yucca and fried green bananas every day. And I can't get the Wangana into my body. It's disgusting!"

Our host Joao welcomes me with a plate of food. Wangana and yucca. I am hungry like never before, and the pale cooked meat and still paler yucca, prepared and presented with such care in an exotic red plastic plate, is without a doubt better than the single cup of rice I have eaten over the last three days.

And it was lovely. Hunger is the best chef. After Joao has supplied me with my third plate of food, which I accept with mixed emotions and a smile, I begin to feel better.

Down The River of Dreadful Turns

Only later does Joe give me the story behind this easy going Indian and his food: the latest victim of Joao's 410 shotgun was a wangana, or wild pig (peccary). These animals are omnivores, eating anything they find, from berries to insects or other mammals. They weigh as much as 40 kilograms and maraud through the woods in troops of up to 50 at a time. They sport dangerous long teeth and can be highly aggressive towards humans.

To preserve the wangana, Joao cut it open, salted it and laid it under palm fronds over a barely live fire, to the great delight of the flies and other bugs. Joe told me how he had seen one of the local watchdogs, of dubious origin, grabbing the wangana's head and running off with it before the host's wife and children were tasked with retrieving this snack from the poor dog.

The slightly chewed head was then placed into one of the aluminum pots and cooked up—to be served to me. These Indians do not have cooling facilities: they can only preserve things by salting and drying them.

A real problem with this process is that in the extremely high humidity, the meat begins to rot during the drying process. And this is the origin of the piquant flavor of their dried wangana. Two days later, the ground has dried enough to allow the Volvo to complete the journey and disgorge its contents at a nearby half built brick building.

Joe still does not feel too well and asks me to ride with them to get the last of the supplies from the Dodge. I take my hunting knife, flashlight, GPS, poncho and necessary medical supplies. Alongside me sits Jorge and Joao.

Jorge passes the time by telling me of the local Indian legends, when a thorn branch sweeps by and whacks him on the cheek. Within seconds the blood flows from the resultant deep cut. Tea tree oil and a plaster are the best I can do, but Jorge looks very pleased, in spite of the considerable pain he must be enduring. Then, out of the blue Jorge asks me: "You tell me you from South Africa... you know Chris Barnard... heart doctor?" Wow, I didn't know the cut on his face was causing this kind of problems...

A Journey through Many Worlds

But luckily Jorge's heart was as good as his general knowledge, and I am astonished at the interesting people that appear out of the blue. Here in the middle of the jungle, I find a man who remembers the name of the South African who performed the first human to human heart transplant in 1967. I am very impressed. We stop at Camp 20, and everyone jumps off the vehicle. "You want to eat? We rest here!", Says Jorge as he gets off, Eat? Rest? No thanks.

It is getting late, and I just want to go and get the damn stuff off the Dodge. Then we can eat and rest. The fat lady receives her guests with gay abandon, and I begin to wonder what her tasks in the camp entail. Only much later do we finally get on the road again.

The road is only slightly drier, and several times we grind to a halt, a few kilometers from Camp 20. We see our stop on the rise and the hopeless driver decides he has had enough. Jorge serves as my interpreter and tells me that we must sleep here for the night. Tomorrow we will try again.

This pushes my patience to its most extreme limit. I do not want to sleep here. I cannot stand their mentality anymore. It is enough! I will walk. Jorge tries to persuade me that some ferocious wild animal will eat me. So be it. Rather that than be trapped here a minute longer with you clowns. And to make things worse, my mosquito net is still on the Dodge. Fuck this.

No, I am going to walk. Jorge regards it as his duty to accompany me, machete at the ready. I guess that we will be there by nightfall. Suddenly Jorge stands dead still. "Snake! I smell!!!" There is a peculiar smell in the air, but we see nothing and continue cautiously. It seems I am becoming accustomed to the forest and its strange noises.

Jorge's experienced eye points out coconas as we walk, and soon we are feasting on them. After what seems to be an eternity, we hear the groan of the Volvo. Once again they have decided to change plan, but this time we are not going to complain.

We climb onto the vehicle and proceed further. It is dark

Down The River of Dreadful Turns

by the time we reach the lonely Dodge. Naturally, no-one has made any provision for light. Fortunately, I have my mini Maglite with me. After two hours of holding my arm above my head, they have loaded over the baggage from the Dodge, and we begin the trek back.

I am elated to think that this is the very last time I will travel up this road which has caused me such pain. I never want to see that road in my life again. In all, I have walked more than 80 kilometers up and down it, between the Dodge and Sawawo. That is enough. For once, everything goes according to plan and late in the evening we drive back into Sawawo.

It turned out to be extremely difficult to get to the Brazilian border. Now we must move still further, and quickly—we have lost much valuable time. Our inquiries tell us that there is, however, no canoe to be bought. No-one can take us to the next town on the Amonea, called Thaumaturgo. But we don't want to get old and die here either.

"We must get out of this place fast," says Joe. As I look at him, he seems to have aged a lot since I first met him nearly six months ago. His eyes look tired, and his face seems very thin. Yes, it sure is time to move.

Our only alternative to a canoe is to build a raft, and with the help of Jorge, we locate a patch of Balsa trees not far from where we sleep. Balsa (Ochroma lagopus) means raft in Spanish because of its excellent buoyancy and is the same wood that is used in building model aircraft. We cut about 12 of these trees with a diameter of around 25 cm (10 inches) and carry them to a patch of open grass next to our hut. Next, we wander off into the jungle to find some lianas which grow plentiful around here. They are very strong rope like plants and prove to be excellent for tying logs together.

By the end of our first day of raft building, we have all the materials ready and cut to size. Tomorrow we can start with the assembly of the vessel.

To the mockery, scorn and nearly protest of the locals, we proceed to start building a raft. They say we are mad and that

A Journey through Many Worlds

the river is impassable on a raft. "Muchos Palos" is a cry we start to recognize. Well, branches or not, we must move. We are nearly finished when someone suddenly offers to sell us a canoe. At only US$60, it is without question a good option. Yes, and the only option besides staying here.

The hollowed out tree trunk is about 7 meters long but very narrow. There is, however, enough space for all our equipment and supplies and for the last time we check the maps: the Amonea river flows right through an Indian territory. Unfortunately, we have no other option. The sores on my body are starting to get worse. At Thaumaturgo there is hopefully a doctor, and this is our only chance.

Today is our last day with Joao and his family. Bird expert Joe Brooks identifies the meal of the day as a type of Curassow. Many species of this crested bird are in imminent danger of becoming extinct, and Joe stares at our host as if a family member has been served up for lunch. He declines to eat the plate of food offered to him and goes and lies down in the hammock. I must say that it was the nicest tasting endangered species I have ever eaten.

A friendly Indian helps us to carry the baggage to the canoe and when we finally depart on 24 August, while a small crowd of Indians stands emotionless on the river bank to see us off. It feels good to know that we are finally reliant upon ourselves for transport. No waiting for a Volvo anymore! We feel a wave of relief as Sawawo disappears behind us.

We paddle a few kilometers further and stop at a beautiful white beach to our right with lots of firewood. Joe starts to make a fire while I put up the tent. After a battle, I manage to catch a catfish with my hand line. I clean it, and it becomes our first of many meals on the river. Our other food supplies are almost finished—we only have lentils and rice left. There are also some lemons we brought from Sawawo, and we use them, along with sugar, to make the brown, yellow river water taste a little bit better.

Early in the morning, we pack away the camp and get the canoe ready once again . The sores on my arms and legs are getting worse by the day.

Down The River of Dreadful Turns

"Muchos Palos" was certainly no exaggeration. Everywhere our path is blocked by branches and trees in and over the river. Sometimes we have to turn round and try and find another route. There are also a million sand banks, visible much too late in the troubled muddy waters of the Amonea. More than once the canoe grinds to a halt in the sand. We must then get out and drag the canoe back into deeper water, or pack out some the equipment to make it lighter. The equipment is then carried over to the river bank where it is once again repacked into the canoe after that has been dragged into deeper water. We waste much time and energy in the process.

Underwater tree stumps are also a hazard: when the canoe hits one of these, its prow locks onto the stump while the current pushes the canoe's rear around. It requires fast reactions and good balance to remain dry in these circumstances.

We drink about one liter of water per person per hour, and there is thus not enough time to purify the water either.

The third day on the Amonea sees us on the lookout for a suitable piece of beach upon which to set up camp. After a wonderful meal of Peruvian lentils and river water (our coffee and sugar have been all used up), we decided to bake some bread as a dessert. Joe gets into the tent to clean his camera, and I observe the six small round pieces of bread start to take on a bit of color over the fire.

Suddenly I see a canoe with three Indians. You don't have to be an expert in body language to see that this was not good news. As they climb out of their canoe, their eyes race over the scene which confronts them.

They first walk over to the canoe and lift up its canvas canopy: the black Busby suitcase and blue steel trunk do not hold their attention, and they approach me, suspicion glowing from their eyes. I instinctively look around for a weapon of any sort. This clearly isn't a social call.

Three paces to my right are my machete with its point stuck into the sand. I feel like I am playing a part in a

A Journey through Many Worlds

Highlander movie. "Joe, I think we've got a problem."

The first mosquito reconnaissance teams are starting to arrive as Joe emerges from the tent, apparently not happy with the interruption to his camera cleaning session. Using the standard mime, mixed with broken Spanish and Portuguese, the leader of the group who has particularly hostile eyes, tells us to come with them. No thank you. We are tired, and the sun is setting. We want to finish eating and then go to sleep. Thank you for the friendly invitation. Perhaps next time? This is the essence of Joe's answers, delivered in a language similar to that which was used originally. Only with a broad fake smile as well.

It does not work. They look even more hostile, and the machete is now rubbing against my leg. Joe, now keen to get some shut eye, repeats his answer, only this time with better expression and unmistakable mimes.

The Indians' aggressive eyes change into bafflement. Joe's plastic on smile remains constant. I also try to stay smiling, but I begin to wonder if maybe it is not such a bad idea, after all, to go with them. I am not keen for a fight so soon after dinner.

In a babble of biblical proportions, the three Indians break out into a furious discussion amongst themselves in their language, and it looks like the leader is about to lose his status. Joe turns around and walks back to his tent—his camera is of course not yet completely clean.

The bread has now begun to smell like a burnt offering, and the Indians, apparently unhappy with the situation, retreat to their canoe still arguing amongst themselves. I pick up the word "amanja" a lot—amanja means 'tomorrow.' Then I recall what Jorge said to me in Sawawo: "You must be careful. Indians call Rio Amonea the "River of dreadful turns."

Top: The Inka Sun Festival, Inti Raymi, Celebrated in Peru. Bottom left: Joe, enjoying "Coca tea." Bottom Middle: Johan with his Karrimor backpack. The same backpack will be used on Expedition Amazon 2017. Next to Johan is Philip Nel. This photo was taken before their 5000 km Cape Town to Mozambique hitch-hiking adventure in 1992 Bottom right: Old indian woman on Lake Titicaca.

A Journey through Many Worlds

Top, below - left & middle: The Magical Machu Picchu, Peru. Bottom right: a Cloud formation on Rio Madeira, Brazil

Top: Rio Jurua, Acre Province, Brazil. Middle left: The mysterious Nazca Lines in Peru. Middle Right: Brightly colored insect, Peru. Bottom left: Rio Jurua. Bottom right: Green Amazon lizzard

A Journey through Many Worlds

Top: Wangana head & Bananas. Middle left: Selling fruit in Lima, Peru. Middle right: Interesting food in Pucallpa, Peru. Bottom left: Cashew Apple & nut, and 2 coconas. Bottom right: Plant used for red paint - The lipstick tree (Bixa orellana)

Top: The red Dodge on the way to Sawawo, Peru. Middle left: Chauchilla Cemetary. Middle right: Silver Piranha. Bottom left: Joe with Canon video camera.
Bottom right: Charging GPS battery with solar panel.

A Journey through Many Worlds

Top: Rio Jurua in Brazil. Bottom left: Indian poses with my Leatherman.
Bottom middle: The famous red haired mummies of Chauchilla, Peru.
Bottom right: Teatro Amazonas in Manaus, Brazil.

Top: Iguana on river bank. Bottom left: "89" Butterfly.
Bottom middle: Sunset on the Jurua.
Bottom right: "El Misti" Volcano, Peru.

A Journey through Many Worlds

Top: Joe Buying a canoe at Sawawo, Peru. Bottom left: Going fishing on Lake Titicaca, Peru. Bottom middle: Traders stock up on the riverbank, Peru. Bottom right: Colorful festival in the Inka Capital, Cuzco.

Top: Pink river dolphin on Rio Jurua. Left middle: Paddling down the Jurua. Left bottom: Skinning a Wangana. Right bottom: An Indian girl in Peru, near Sawawo.

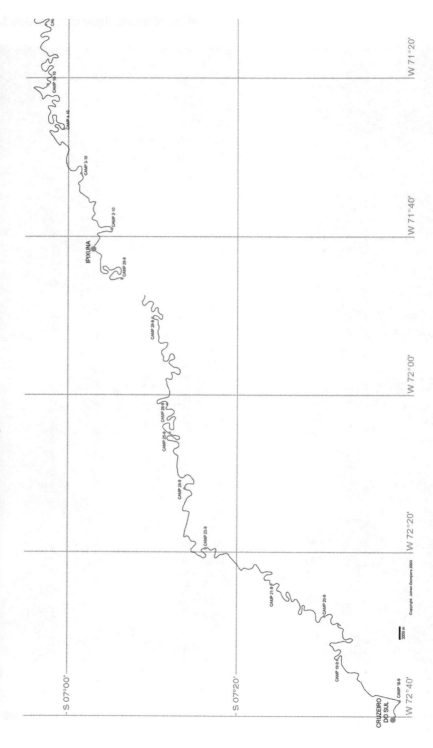

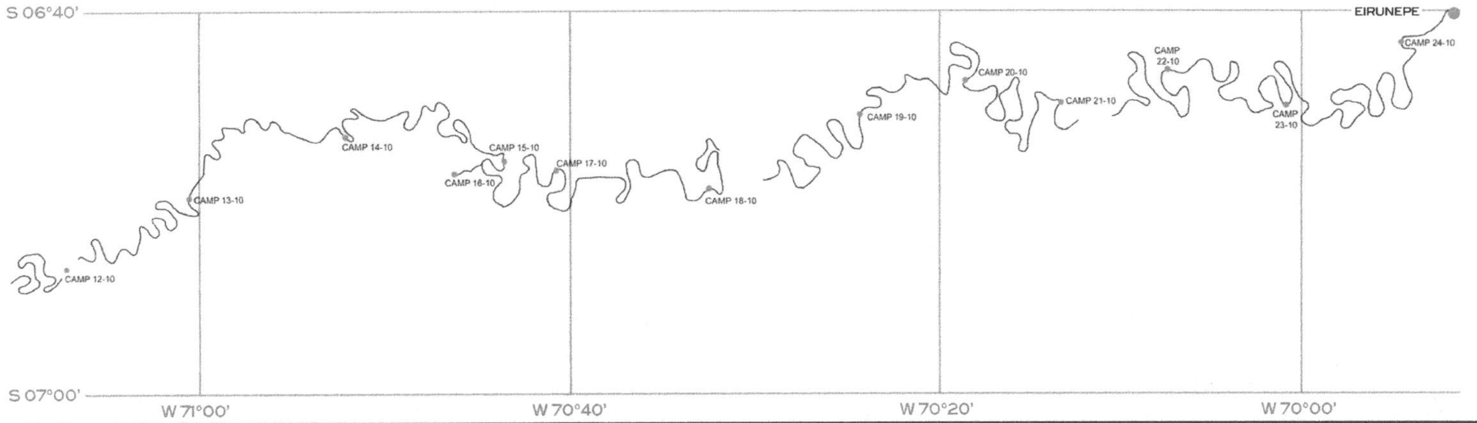

S 06°40'

EIRUNEPE

CAMP 24-10

CAMP 23-10

CAMP 22-10

CAMP 21-10

CAMP 20-10

CAMP 19-10

CAMP 18-10

CAMP 17-10

CAMP 15-10

CAMP 16-10

CAMP 14-10

CAMP 13-10

CAMP 12-10

S 07°00'

W 71°00'   W 70°40'   W 70°20'   W 70°00'

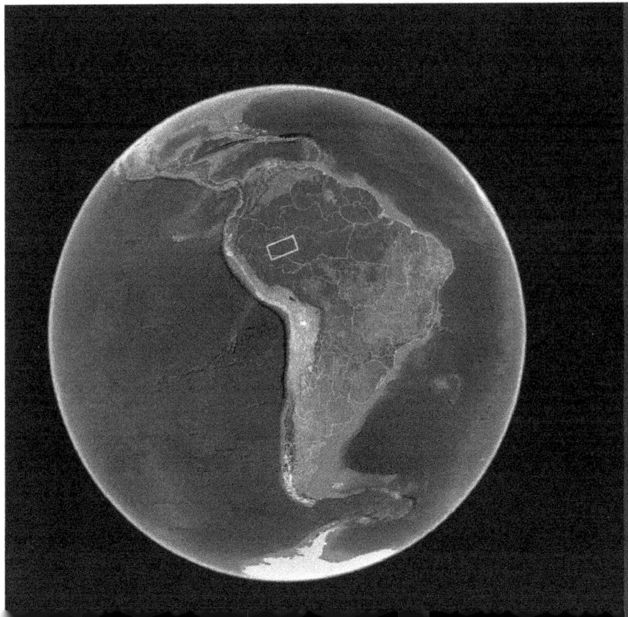

Copyright Google Earth

A Journey through Many Worlds

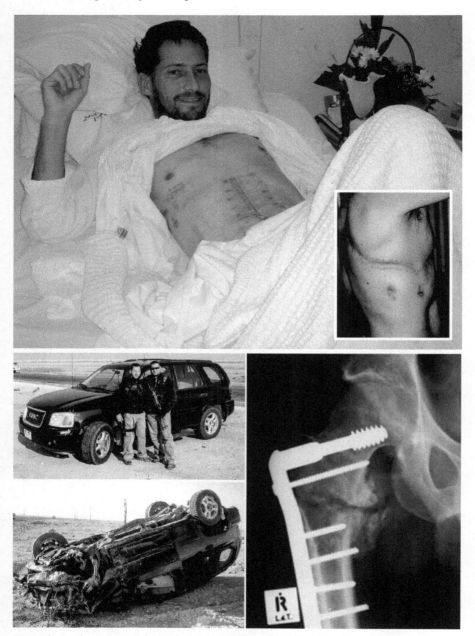

Top: The author, drugged and happy to be alive. Middle left: Johan & Ziad with GMC Envoy. Bottom Left: GMC Envoy after the incident. Bottom right: Broken femur - a dynamic condylar hip screw implant was done at a Kuwait City hospital.

Top: Landing at Bamyan, Afghanistan. 2nd left: Johan, Major H and Bryan "Snakehips" Donaldson, (ex Selous Scout). 3rd left Pilot Basmah and Johan before doing aerial photos in Wadi Rum, Jordan. Right top: Bosnian friend & team member, Llubisa (Killed in Action). Right bottom: Winter street scene, Kabul, Afghanistan.

A Journey through Many Worlds

Top left: Coming down from "The Monastry" at Petra, Jordan. Top right: The Treasury, Petra, Jordan. Bottom left: Security Manager, Gurkha, and good friend Hem Bahadur Rai, Kabul, Afghanistan. Bottom right: 2 Young Afghan soldiers, Kabul, Afghanistan 2007

Top: Longest fuel convoy on earth - we did the protection of convoys, sometimes of more than 300 petrol tankers in Iraq.
Bottom left: Tyson & Johan eating lobster they received as rations from the United States Air Force base at Talil, Iraq.
Bottom right: One of our Iraqi Protection Force guards stand guard near Nasseriyah.

A *Journey through Many Worlds*

Top: Aerial view of Kabul, Afghanistan. Bottom left: Street children, Kabul. Middle right: Johan as operations officer. Bottom right: Dr Munther Zureigat at the Serena Hotel in Kabul, shortly before several people were killed in a suicide attack at the hotel.

Top: Ziggurat at Ur, Iraq. Johan, second from left, Joe Bresler (Former Rhodesian SAS & Selous Scout, Killed in Action), Jeff Waters, 'Bones' Greeff & 3 Korean soldiers in uniform. Middle left: LOI Team, Iraq. Bottom Left: Radar dish on the Kuwait/Iraq border. Bottom right: Italians, Iraq.

Top: A team depart for an attack, Saurimo, Angola. Middle & bottom left: Johan working for Executive Outcomes, Angola. Bottom right: Johan after completing 2 years military service, including Operation Hooper, Angola.

Chapter 12
Captured by Campa Indians—
The Chief has Spoken

Loss of liberty is a human disaster and to have liberty taken away is to be caught up in a process which, completed, encompasses the beginnings and ends of human life.

—Song Lin

In the morning, we load up our canoe, and by six o'clock we are already paddling down the river. It is an unusually hot day, and the humidity rises quickly. By midday, we hear the drone of a motor, and around the next corner, we see a traditional Indian canoe, powered by a less traditional Yamaha outboard motor. The Indian canoe slows down and chugs alongside us. At the helm is our friend from the previous evening, accompanied by his two colleagues. They all look as unfriendly as before—maybe even worse. "Amanja" has come. With renewed put-on smiles, which are not returned, we row on, a little faster.

The three musketeers disappear behind us. I bend over to plot our position on the GPS—South 9°10'13, West 72°54'56.7. I instinctively know that this can be an important piece of information—if somebody should ever find the GPS...

The Indians appear to be dropping back; their motor becomes fainter against the buzzing of the insects. But, just as it is about to be completely drowned out, they pick up speed again. Their canoe creeps alongside ours, and the forward Indian throws a rope across our bow. The middle one

A Journey through Many Worlds

clutches a bow and arrow, and looks decidedly unfriendly, with red stripes daubed across his face. Their more powerful boat drags us across the symbolically troubled waters of the Amonea.

We can do nothing, and with mixed emotions, we watch as the leader of this hijack points in the direction in which we are going. Some time later I can see in front of us a wisp of white smoke that runs up from between the trees to mix with the grey-white thunderclouds above.

Our unfriendly companions tie both ends of our canoes to a wooden pole on the left-hand side of the river. Alongside are another two canoes. We are instructed, by hand signals, to climb up the five-meter river bank. Worn out mud steps are barely visible, and we make the ascent with great difficulty, sliding barefoot here and there, followed by the Indians. A painful exercise for me to ascend the bank. What can we expect next in this Indian territory?

Joe and I are quiet. We have no idea what will unfold now. All around us, more Indians appear from nowhere, some clutching bows and arrows, and none of them look friendly. We are lead along a footpath, which leads past several open plan huts and trees, before being instructed to enter a particular hut. It is on poles, has wooden walls and one entrance.

By this time, the pain in my left leg has become unbearable, and I am forced to sit suddenly on the floor. Three insect bites just above my ankle have turned septic, and the red inflammation in the surrounding tissue has become a throbbing pain. Apart from a few wooden planks and a wooden rack in one corner, the hut is empty. A hole in the floor provides a view onto the grass below, where I see a chicken pecking at the ground.

A wooden chair—something I have not yet seen amongst any Indians—is carried into the hut. Then a well built man, dressed in a long dark brown caftan, enters the hut. Around his neck he wears a necklace of beads, palm seeds and Toucan feathers. He looks like a caricature of an Indian chief, Sitting Bull or something. He has a stately appearance—his

Captured by Campa Indians

movement is even slow and considered. He looks at us for a moment with penetrating eyes, and then takes up the seat. At his side stands a thinner man garbed in similar apparel. In the meantime, the group of observers standing outside has grown to about 50, of who most wear the same type of brown clothing.

The interrogation begins. Joe tries his best to understand and Sitting Bull looks singularly unimpressed at our presence in his kingdom. How much they ever understood of Joe's explanation of who we were and what we were doing, is anybody's guess.

In between the questions are extended periods of silence during which we are just observed. In answer to Joe's question if they could offer us any medical help, the simple answer was "Nao". Sand Flies now buzz around my open sores like they have found the last oasis in the desert.

After a long, and in my opinion, fruitless discussion, Sitting Bull arises and walks over to the other end of the hut where our baggage has been thrown down in a heap. The great search now begins. Eager hands rip open our bags and suitcases. The entire Indian community seems compelled to take part in this process.

I pity Joe greatly as he tries to explain to the Indians what the sun panels, GPS, Motorola cell phone and other technological miracles actually are. An Indian with a particularly unpleasant face grabs a fold up reflector and starts to take it out of its holder.

Joe wants to explain but I stop him. Call it my idea of revenge. In a moment, the reflector pops open to its full size. The wide eyed Indian is astonished. Now I indicate to him to put in back into its container.

Of course he has no idea how to do this, as unless you know how, it is indeed an impossible task to put the big reflector back into its small holder. Waiting until he has made himself look ridiculous in front of his peers, I take the reflector and with a quick twist, drop it back in its container. He slinks away.

131

A Journey through Many Worlds

More than an hour later, Sitting Bull is finished with his inspection and his subordinates leave the hut, moving outside to stare at their strange visitors once again. "We must wait here," translates Joe, repeating the order given to him.

"Wait for what, and for how long Joe?"

"I don't know."

"Shit shit shit."

We pack the baggage back into the bags and sit down to discuss our lack of options, under the constant gaze of several pairs of Indian eyes.

"Well, I don't know about you Johan, but I didn't see any human sized pots outside," remarks Joe, somewhat dryly.

"Sure Joe, but with my luck, this bloody tribe is a bit more advanced, maybe they will first chop their victims up before cooking them in smaller pots."

The truth is that we are so thin that no Indian or cannibal with any self-respect will take the trouble to eat us—even the black vultures had stopped looking in our direction. (Fortunately at this stage we had not heard of Col Leonard Clark's story of an unfortunate man by the name of Rodriguez. He was apparently a thin and mean gold prospector, who ignored warnings about the cannibalistic Campa Indians by replying that he was too thin and that they would never be interested in eating him. Poor Rodriguez then vanished, and only much later did a captured Indian tell what had happened to him. The Campas had caught the over confident thin man. He had been castrated and kept for months in a small cell while being fed. As apparently one of the side effects of castration is weight gain. After he had put on enough weight, he was butchered and eaten).

Medical help and food were our single biggest priorities, and Joe took it upon himself to try and negotiate something with our captors.

We still did not know what their plan with us was, and apart from Sitting Bull and his thin colleague, there was

Captured by Campa Indians

no-one else who could speak anything even remotely understandable.

GPS in hand, I plotted our position on the map. As the Macaw flies, Thaumaturgo is only about 30 kilometers north east of our current position, and the only way to get there is by canoe or raft.

According to all indications, there was a doctor there. The bad news was that our canoe, along with the others, was now in the hands of the Indians. There are no roads in the area, and if you tried to cut open a footpath, you would be presented with several months' work.

The vegetation is so thick that in many places you cannot even see a meter in front of you. After a while, a woman with strongly discernible Western features enters the hut. She is the first one here to show any sort of emotion. She carries a tray with three small fish and some yucca and puts it on the floor. Joe thanked her and used the chance to ask if she had any medicine for the open sores.

Minutes later, she came back with a red liquid and indicated that we rub it on the wounds. "Muito Obrigado," I thanked her. Please just let it work. The sand flies were now making it unbearable for me, and after putting up our hammocks, I put up the tent in the hut and went and lay down inside.

It made no difference which position I adopted, the sores on my arms and legs remained in contact with the sleeping bag underneath me, and I would wake up in pain at regular intervals. "Come and have some coffee, Johan. " Slowly I open my eyes, No, it was not a bad dream, but even worse reality.

We were still the 'guests' of a tribe of red faced, unfriendly Indians. Joe had obtained coffee and sugar from the woman who had earlier brought us food. He had boiled the water on a fire opposite our hut. (Three tree trunks had been put together in such a way that they made a sort of star formation. A fire was made at the points, and as these logs burned shorter and shorter, the logs are pushed inwards, so

A Journey through Many Worlds

the three points stay together. In this way, one could keep a fire going for very long time if necessary.)

Joe slept in his hammock and told me that when he opened his eyes, he found himself surrounded by a group of expressionless faces observing him from every angle. It was evident that they did not often have guests. In the one corner of the hut was a small type of wooden rack, in which lay a white cloth.

Upon closer inspection, I saw that it was not just a piece of cloth, but in fact a pair of underpants: Calvin Klein underpants!

"That probably belonged to the last idiot who tried to go down the Amonea river," says Joe. "God knows where the rest of him is."

The rest of him was definitely not in the hut, and we decide that it probably was clever not to make inquiries about our late yuppie predecessor. Certain things are better left untold.

My leg was, however, getting worse and worse, and if I tried to lie or sit and then stand up, it felt like the whole limb was going to burst open from the pressure and pain. In desperation, I had now tried everything in the medical supply kit, from Tea tree oil to Voltaren Gel and even foot powder—but nothing helped. There were now 28 septic sores all over my arms and legs. The red liquid also had no effect at all.

I looked once again at our maps and with the GPS, tried to think of a way out of this appalling situation. Most of the day I sheltered in the tent in an attempt to stay out of the way of the sand flies and other insects. Although I felt like a Jaguar with a sore tooth, I was pretty angry at being trapped in a cage like an animal at the zoo.

Mother Theresa, who earlier brought us food, arrived once again at about midday to check on the patient/prisoners. By the way, she acted, it seems as if she was not even supposed to have contact with us. Joe tells her very diplomatically that if I do not get some medical supplies soon, my condition will get substantially worse and that I may just get my final

Captured by Campa Indians

resting place here amongst the Indians. It seems as if this prospect upsets her greatly, and after a quick inspection of the wounds, she disappears once again.

The dark night which follows is even worse than the previous one, and I sleep very little. I am not hungry or thirsty, but everything irritates me immensely. Joe tries hard to cheer me up, but I do not appreciate his efforts at all. If I could only find a way of getting some relief from this burning pain. . . .

In one of the nearby huts, I hear someone playing what sounds like a pan flute, interrupted now and then by what sounds like a baby screaming after being placed in hot water.

The morning of the third day with the Campas appears to start as awfully as the others, but Mother Theresa arrives and tells us that she has a message. It has something to do with Thaumaturgo, and it seems as if we are to be put back on our way. Joe disappears from the hut and comes back with a broad smile. He says he has found where the Indians have hidden our canoe, just a short way away. He has brought it back to its original mooring place, he says.

Shortly afterward an excited Indian rushes into the hut and begins babbling about a canoe. In a few nearly understandable Portuguese words, he is trying to tell us that we cannot take it. Joe answers him with his unique non-verbal fuck-you smile.

At midday, a few more Indians enter the hut and indicate that we must take up our baggage and come with them, Once again, Thaumaturgo is named. Even though my leg is excruciatingly painful, I help to pack up, and a short while later we are back at the canoe with our baggage. The farewell party of onlookers continues to grow all the while. Joe pulls our canoe closer, and we start to load our baggage into it. It looks like we are away!

Sitting Bull's thin lieutenant suddenly appears and informs us that we cannot take our canoe. Why not? I wonder. Suddenly things turn very nasty. The Indians nearest to us start grabbing our baggage and run with surprising ease up

A Journey through Many Worlds

the muddy riverbank and away. The thin lieutenant grabs Joe's backpack, but the wily old man has a grip on it, and it turns into a wrestling match. They pull it to and fro with each combatant screaming at each other in their own language. The Indian shouts over his shoulder and more Indians come to his aid, hesitantly climbing down to the riverside.

"Joe, leave it!" I yell. "It's my bloody backpack!" Joe replies, still struggling with the Indian. Hobbling around on my sore leg, I am unable to have a real go at any of the Indians, but I am furious and feel a strong urge to kill Sitting Bull and his gangsters in a creative way.

But our situation is, of course, hopeless—we are heavily outnumbered, have no weapons, most of our baggage has now been stolen, and all Joe is fighting over is one rucksack. We decide to call a halt to our struggles, and together with the Indians, climb back up the riverbank.

We are shepherded back to our hut, where we sit for a long time in silence, with desperation, disappointment, and anger brewing up inside. The thin lieutenant enters the shelter and gives us our sleeping goods back. The rest of the baggage, however, is not returned.

I once again set up the tent and lay down inside it—too angry to think or do anything else. After yet another uneasy night, Mother Theresa arrives once again in the morning, this time, to my amazement, with a primitive medical kit. There are bandages and an ointment of some sort. She cleans my sores one by one and bandages them up. After an hour or so she is finished, and she leaves after observing her patient, who now looks and feels like an Egyptian mummy.

Even if her machinations have not relieved the pain, I at least feel slightly better as a result of the personal attention and the fact that the wounds are now clean.

A large yellow and blue Macaw announces our fourth day of captivity with a loud shriek. He joins the ever present group of curious onlookers outside our hut, and after a short while decides that he must come into the hut to have a closer look. How about that, I think, even the animals are coming

136

Captured by Campa Indians

to view us. Ever since I was bitten through the ear by a parrot at home, I have been petrified of large birds, and this Macaw has a terribly large and nasty looking beak.

Fortunately the Macaw does not torture me for long with his presence and flies out to go and sit in one of the trees near the river. Just outside our hut, we find a big bunch of bananas—has someone left it there for us?

Later, Mother Theresa brings more food for us, yucca and beans. My eye catches the white Calvin Klein underpants, and my appetite vanishes.

By the sixth day, we are utterly desperate and downhearted. Will we ever get out of this nightmare? What is going to happen next? Are they cannibals? Is this how it will all end? Joe's attempts to negotiate further with the Indians are hopeless.

We have now thought of all the possibilities, including 'stealing' our canoe and setting off in the middle of the night—but that will mean losing all our equipment. I am also in pain and very slow moving at the moment. The thought of poison arrow darts in my back and ass is not an encouraging thought.

This prospect is unthinkable, and we are discussing it when we hear a commotion in the village. Voices are everywhere, and I hear calling in what sounds like Portuguese.

Three people come walking across an open piece of field. In the middle is Senhor Renato, police chief from Thaumaturgo, dressed in camouflage pants, gray shirt, bullet proof vest and a pair of white sneakers. On either side of the police chief are members of Brazilian Policia Militar, sporting Belgian FN automatic assault rifles and facial expressions which look like Rambo, just before he killed his 34th straight opponent. I am unsure if we should be happy or terrified.

It seems like most of the Campas have shown a clean pair of heels, and only a few of the tribal leaders stand and observe from a distance. After Senhor Renato has quickly talked with Sitting Bull's lieutenant, other Indians emerge from their

A Journey through Many Worlds

hiding places, carrying pieces of our stolen baggage. Joe says he wants our canoe back, but Renato says no.

"Vamos. Vamos Rapido!" is his advice: "Go, quickly."

He tells Joe we are not going to row on this river again and that worries me a bit as if he knows something we do not. The police's motorized canoe is almost eight meters long. Joe and I are ordered to sit in the middle with our baggage, while Renato and one of the Rambo clones sit in front. Rambo II and the skipper take up the rear.

The open hostility with which we are viewed by both the Indians and the police makes me wonder if this adventure is going to end up even more spectacularly than it has begun. Every movement is watched and as I take a pack of cigarettes out of my returned backpack, I wonder what our fate is to be. There are only three cigarettes left, I note.

We leave the Indian settlement, and for several hours and about 150 kilometers of the trip, we say nothing. The Amonea River becomes broader and more and more settlements appear on the banks. At places, the forest has been leveled to reveal open grass fields. It gets dark, but the police boat continues at a constant speed, the experienced skipper not flinching as visibility declines.

Every few seconds Renato switches on his flashlight for a short while, using batteries which should have been replaced a long time ago. There are places where branches or other obstacles lurk in the water—if we hit one of them at this speed, it will all be over very quickly.

Around a corner, the lights of Thaumaturgo appear. Instinctively I feel a smile spread across my face. It feels good to be back in civilization, even if it seems as if tonight we might have to sleep in police cells. The canoe is moored to a low wooden jetty, and while I get up all stiff and sore, Renato starts chatting to Joe.

"Johan, he wants us to book in at the local hotel!" says Joe. "What? Are you serious? I thought we were under arrest or something!"

138

Captured by Campa Indians

"But the best part is they said that they are flying us to Cruzeiro do Sul tomorrow." It is incredible to think how our situation has changed over the last 24 hours. From total desperation in the hands of hostile Indians to the luxuries of a jungle town with electricity!

Our new abode is a room in the wooden Hotel Cristiano, on the third floor. There is a single bed, also a place for a hammock, an electric fan and billions of mosquitoes. We store our baggage and venture into the streets in search of something to eat.

The only option is an open air grill room or churrascaria. Here we buy some barbecued steak, Farinha de mandioca (manioc flour), and beans. This is a fantastic meal, and it is rounded off with a beer. If only there were beautiful women here, I could have mistaken it for Valhalla.

The next day, Thursday 3 September, Senhor Renato knocks on our door. "Vamos, Vamos" is once again his first words. He sounded like the corporal I had when I did my military service as if he has the need to sound like he is in a hurry all the time.

Nonetheless, we pack hastily and follow Renato to his house, a short distance from the hotel. Here he loses his militant image and in a moment of weakness (or perhaps because he was not in front of his troops) he offers us real bread, butter, and coffee. "Vamos! Vamos!" however soon follows, and we, along with a batch of unhappy looking porters are transported across the river by canoe. From here it is a few minutes walk to the cement runway of Thaumaturgo airport.

At exactly 08h00 the six seater Federal Police aircraft touches down as I watch with barely suppressed excitement. This must be one of the one or two times that anything happened on time during the entire trip.

But then again, maybe the timing of the aircraft was a coincidence. Federal agents Alexander Antonio Estrela Mechetti and Fabio Setsuo Ogata introduce themselves in very clear American English accents.

A Journey through Many Worlds

Both are dressed in the black t-shirts of "Policia Federal" which have that name in bold yellow letters on their backs. Ogata, a third generation Japanese Brazilian, has an Austrian Glock 19 9mm pistol strapped firmly to his leg and the thin Mechetti's Glock is normally holstered on his right side. Senhor Renato exchanges a few words with the federal agents and a few minutes later our baggage is loaded into the aircraft.

Ogata sits next to the pilot, and Mechetti sits between Joe and me. The plane quickly gathers speed, takes off and banks sharply to the left in the direction of Cruzeiro do Sul.

From 3500 feet, the Jurua looks like an enormous anaconda winding its way through a surrounding mat of long dark green rainforest tree cover. During the flight, the two policemen talk animatedly, and we begin to feel more confident that they are well disposed towards us after all. They ask us again and again about the Indians and tell us that we were very lucky to get out of there alive and unhurt.

Less than an hour later we land at Cruzeiro do Sul (meaning "Southern Cross") international airport. Cruzeiro do Sul has 67,000 inhabitants and is the second largest city in the Brazilian province of Acre. The climate is scorching, with high humidity and a rainfall averaging between 2000 and 2500 mm per year.

To bring that into perspective, the average annual rainfall for Cape Town is 213 mm, London 597 mm and for New York, it is 618 mm per year.

Its economy is mainly based on rubber and Brazil nut production. Acre originally belonged to Bolivia, but seeing as the majority of the inhabitants were Brazilians, the region was occupied by Brazil at the beginning of the 20th Century after civil disturbances sparked off by tax impositions by the Bolivian government.

As we taxi in, I see a luxury 4x4 vehicle with flashing red and blue lights and a big federal police badge on the side approach. All our baggage gets loaded into the car, and the driver takes us to a restaurant near the center of town. It is

140

Captured by Campa Indians

a pleasant, clean place, decorated in bright colors and after a hearty meal, we depart for the headquarters of the Policia Federal.

The 4x4 passes through a large steel gate attached to a white building with high antennas. Behind the building, several other vehicles stand, including a camouflaged aluminum speed boat.

"So you are the South African and the Englishman?" asks the blond haired man with intelligent eyes. He is dressed in civilian clothes, and it seems as if he is in charge.

"That's right, and you are?" I ask, extending my hand.

"Ramitez De Almeida" introduces himself with a firm handshake.

"You are in charge here?" I ask.

"No, not really, but please bring your luggage inside," he answers evasively.

The general police attitude is one of professionalism and in no way aggressive. We walk into the building and after passing several offices, reach a wooden door with a notice on it: "Nucleo de Operandi."

Inside the office are three desks with computers and we are requested to put our baggage down on the floor. We draw chairs closer, and Ramitez asks us to tell him exactly what happened, while the other officials stand around listening.

Now and then he interrupts our narrative and asks something, and after we have finished, he leaves the room for a few minutes and returns with another agent armed with a video camera.

"Unfortunately we need to search your luggage, do you mind?" Ramitez says, in a manner which makes us feel as if we actually have a choice.

Without waiting for an answer, they start with Joe's baggage and unpack everything carefully, all the time looking for any potential secret compartments. They photocopy Joe's Dairy. While this goes on, Ramitez chats with me.

141

A Journey through Many Worlds

"So why did you enter Brazil on the Amonea river?" he asks.

"Well, we didn't have any other option at that stage—we were stuck in Sawawo, couldn't turn back due to heavy rains and mostly impassable roads, and above all, we needed medical attention."

"Were you aware that you entered an indigenous Indian area?"

"Sure! It's indicated on our map as an indigenous area, but we didn't have any other options."

"Senhor, you know that not even the federal police enters that area unless it's really necessary. It's wild country, and nasty things can happen there. There were cases when we had to go to retrieve bodies from indigenous areas. People get killed, and the Indians are seen as minors under the Brazilian law," Ramitez says, his penetrating eyes narrowing slightly. "For who are you working?" he continues.

"As we've told you, we are photographing and exploring the Jurua river. We are not working for somebody. We are doing it independently."

"Sorry, but it's hard to believe—look at all your equipment! Satellite navigation, hi tech film equipment—and you've got better maps of the area than the Federal Police!" he says.

"Well, we just did our best with planning and preparing because we did not have any reliable information about what we will find here. I'm telling you we are just two photographers on an expedition," I reply, feeling a little bit worried now. We break for lunch, and Ramitez drops us off at a nearby restaurant where we enjoy a typical Brazilian meal consisting of meat, spaghetti, beans, rice and so on. At least we are not locked up, and I must say these people are very professional.

Back at the office, my baggage gets searched next. It, of course, delivers nothing of interest to the police, and Ramitez then continues his interrogation.

"Maybe you are bio-pirates?", he asks out of the blue.

142

Captured by Campa Indians

"What?" I reply.

"You must know the term! Scientists come from foreign countries to take specimen from Amazonia for foreign research on medicine. In that way, Brazil loses millions each year. Because they steal from our rich biological heritage, we call them bio-pirates."

"Look, in our present condition we may look a bit like pirates, but do we look like the scientist type?" Or did you find any specimens in our luggage?" is the best answer I can think of. It seems to have the desired effect on Ramitez, and he appears to give up on his quest to find something wrong with us.

He then turns the conversation to logging: "So did you spot any suspicious or logging related activities on your travels?"

Of course, we did! We rode with the loggers, and for all practical purposes, Sawawo is nothing but a big logging camp. With the aid of the GPS I can give him the exact locations of the spots, and he makes photocopies of our maps.

It is up to the federal police to decide what they are going to do with the information. We also don't have any idea about who has licenses to do what. He tells us that there are problems with Peruvian loggers who chop down trees in Brazilian territory and then drag the logs over the border before the Brazilian police can get there.

These trees are then moved by truck to Nuevo Italia from where they are taken via the Ucayali or one of its tributaries, to Pucallpa. Most of the wood lost in this manner is Cedar and Mahogany.

Later that afternoon, Ramitez decides that he is finished with us for the day. He and Ogata will take us to our hotel and tomorrow they will continue with their questioning. We ask them when they will they be done with us, and Ramitez answers that he is following instructions from the provincial headquarters in Rio Branco. In other words, he does not know. Joe is starting to look a bit weak, and I ask if it is possible for him to stay in the room the next day

143

A Journey through Many Worlds

while I come in for further questioning. Ramitez agrees it is better for Joe to rest. It is Brazil's presidential election, and as a result accommodation in Cruzeiro is scarce. An extended search result in Ogata finding accommodation in a hotel at the bargain price R$20 per night. The room has air conditioning, no windows, a color TV, a bathroom and even place to hang up clothes.

We are exhausted after the mentally taxing day and soon collapse into a deep sleep.

Day two of the interrogation is more informal, and while I wait for the senior officers in Rio Branco to decide on our fate, I get to know Ramitez better. He tells me that he lived in the United States as a Mormon for a few years before he joined the police.

Then he strikes out on an unusual course: "Please tell me about the Boer War in South Africa."

This one surprises me: I didn't know that police training in Brazil included universal history!

"How the hell did you know about that?" I ask, very impressed.

"My name is Ramitez Vozniak de Almeida," he answers, triumphantly.

"Yes, and...?"

"My mother was Russian, and as a little boy she gave me a book by Jules Verne called 'The Adventures of 3 Englishmen and 3 Russians in South Africa'. The six men and their Bushman guide did meridian measurements in a South African desert when war broke out between England and Russia. That made me interested in your country's history, and I also know that many Russians fought with the Boers against England."

This is the last thing I expected to be discussing here, from an American trained Brazilian Mormon policeman with a Russian mother living in the Amazon. But then again, this is a world full of surprises. After an interesting discussion stretching over several continents, Ogata interrupts us.

144

Captured by Campa Indians

"I have some bad news," he says. Shit, that doesn't sound good. Just don't say they are going to take our films. Rather deport us.

"Unfortunately we must confiscate the seeds," he says.

"The seeds? What seeds?" I ask surprised. I have of course completely forgotten about the little bottle of seeds I picked in Sawawo. My idea was to give it to a girlfriend back home, as she likes to work with such things and make necklaces and other stuff.

"Please, be my guest! My only request is to have a statement of the confiscation," I say, once they show the bottle and remind me.

"And you need to process the films that were taken in Brazil," Ogata continues.

"I need to process it?" I repeat.

"Yes, it's the instructions from Rio Branco." This is not the worst thing that can happen, I decide. The only problem is that they are slide transparency film which cannot be developed in Cruzeiro do Sul.

Ogata has a solution to this, however. "We will send it off by airplane to Rio Branco, and you will have it back in two days. But you need to pay for the processing up front, those are my orders," he says.

"Tell your boss that I'll pay half of the cost if they don't fuck up my films," I reply.

"You don't understand; my boss is a very difficult person."

I decide that the situation can be exploited a little bit more, as I don't really know if they are lying to me in an attempt to boost their salary for this month a bit. I play my trump card: "No deal," I reply with a straight face. "Your boss wants it processed, so to be nice; I'll pay 50% only when I get my film back."

Ogata and Ramitez exchange a few words in Portuguese, and then Ramitez turns to me and says "We don't want further trouble, so we will pay for it upfront."

145

A Journey through Many Worlds

Something tells they are telling the truth. "That's fine, thank you," I say, feeling a little bit sorry at my effrontery. Ramitez says he will inform us as soon as the films are back. After they have completed the entire statement of what has happened to us, they make a copy of it to give to Joe and I and stamp our passports which I remembered to bring with me.

Before I leave, I visit the restaurant around the corner once more and order a "Fillet de Carvalho"—horse fillet. I have always wanted to try this meal, and I am not disappointed as the meat is succulent and juicy.

Back at the hotel, I find Joe still in bed. He says that he has rested well and the news that the police are now finished with us makes him considerably more relaxed.

Ramitez goes out of his way to make our stay in Cruzeiro as comfortable as possible. At the local offices of Varig, the Brazilian airline, he introduces us to a clerk who can speak English.

The blond man offers us Internet access, and I can send an SMS to my girlfriend to call me at the Varig offices. When I hear her voice a few minutes later, it sounds very strange. The conversation is stilted, and the fact that we talk via satellite (with the resultant time delay) makes things even more challenging. I tell her quickly what has happened, and that we are now safe again.

I ask her to get Arthur to call us at the hotel so that I can update him as well. When I put down the telephone, I suddenly realize how much my life has become involved with this expedition.

The past few weeks have seen me forget entirely about the outside world, and focus only on our survival. The conversation pulls me back to the world from which I came, and I realize that it is not quite as nice as I expected it to be.

Chapter 13
Recovering under the Southern Cross

"Life is like a game of cards. The hand you are dealt is determanism; the way you play it is free will.."

—J.R.R. Tolkien

I phone Arthur from our hotel, and he is surprised, to say the least, to find out what has happened to us. He undertakes to issue a press release to the media on the events, and within an hour the phone rings—Richard Thomson from the South African Press Association (SAPA) is on the line. While we are talking, a thunderstorm erupts, and it begins to rain so fiercely that I can barely hear what Richard is saying. He says the story is very newsworthy and that SAPA will immediately issue a press alert. After this, the story spreads like wildfire amongst the South African media and the telephone rings constantly.

The next day, Monday 9 September, we appear on the front page of the Cape Times in South Africa and also in numerous other papers throughout the country. The South African television service features the story prominently on their main news bulletins, and a well known Sunday newspaper calls me for an interview. A few days later Arthur tells me that there was even coverage in the UK and that through the Internet the story has created waves all over the world. E-mails start pouring in, and more radio stations and magazines ask for interviews.

A Journey through Many Worlds

But the days creep slowly past at our guesthouse. We take it easy, and each morning at 11h00 we visit the restaurant Napolitana across the street for an ala carte feast at a very affordable price. We know we must regain strength as soon as possible. We are only at the beginning of our journey. They have all sorts of meat, fish, and chicken, salads, potatoes, and rice—more than one man can eat. Your plate is then weighed, and you pay according to the weight. Clever. After a couple of days, the staff at the restaurant pick upon our routine, and when we walk in, a glass of coke and ice already awaits us at our table. Joe's favorite is ice cream as dessert. Cruzeiro is a heavenly oasis after our recent experiences.

Ramitez (he pronounces his name as "Ham-and-cheese") awaits us in our hotel room when we get back from town. "We received your films back, but there are no images on it!" he says, pulling out a sheet of blank negatives from an envelope.

The emulsion is completely gone, and I can't tell with any degree of certainty if it is even the same film which I gave to him initially. Most likely it has been 'developed' using the wrong chemical process.

"It's fucked up!" "I can't believe it! They fucked it up!"

Ramitez looks at a loss and starts talking with Joe about the stress of his profession. As I calm down, I realize it is actually not so bad after all. At least we have our camera equipment, and the rest of the film survived the past few weeks.

Even if it was grossly negligent, the loss of two films is not the end of the world. But they would have been good pictures. A new crisis emerges: our cash is now at an end, and we visit the Banco do Brasil to draw some more. We must buy another canoe and food to continue our journey, after all.

The only person who can talk English at the bank is Daniella, a beautiful dark haired girl with a body that makes me long for home. She is, without a doubt, the most beautiful person I have seen in months, and when she tells us that she comes from Rio de Janeiro, I seriously consider launching

Recovering under the Southern Cross

our next expedition from that city.

However, Daniella is also the one to tell us that our bank cards will not work in Cruzeiro. The town is cut off from the modern world, and the only way for us to get any money is via Western Union. Oh, but there is another alternative: we could travel to Acre's capital, Rio Branco—almost 650 kilometers southeast of Cruzeiro. I call a friend in South Africa to find out where the nearest Western Union branch to her is, only to discover that Western Union no longer operates from that country.

We then call on Bob Webb in the USA, who traveled the Amazon River with Joe some four decades previously, and he promises to send us some money via Western Union. Within 30 minutes, Daniella hands over our money. "Be careful on your crazy adventure, and please e-mail me some photos!" is her parting greeting.

For a moment I reflect on how interesting it is that somehow at precisely the right moment, people appear on the scene which makes you think it is all worth it after all.

Brazilian TV is interesting: I am busy watching a show about their presidential election. The bearded left winger Lula da Silva is the favorite to win the fourth democratic election to be held since the 21-year military dictatorship ended in 1985.

Joe is busy drawing up a list of supplies we still need to buy, as I, with one eye on the TV, pour myself another glass of aguardiente and chuckle at the adventure so far. Then suddenly everything is dead quiet and pitch black. The tropical storm that has been raging outside has cut the power.

As I grope for my Petzl flashlight, the lack of air-conditioning makes our room stuffy within a manner of minutes. I hear Joe's voice in the darkness: "Great! A power failure! All I need. Now all the bloody ice cream will melt!" He is very attached to his ice cream; I think it is his lifeline to civilization, I think my lifeline is meat.

Dr Juan Carlos Correa Celi, Cruzeiro's sole pediatrician,

A Journey through Many Worlds

has been supplying us with good medicine, and we are quickly fully on the road to recovery. The antibiotics work wonders on the open sores on my arms and legs, and they are now brown scars rather than gaping holes.

The time has come to get a canoe and carry on with this venture. A small village of wooden huts is about a half hour walk from our hotel. It lies on the banks of the Jurua River, and as we walk on the ground road between the huts, the locals glare at us. Beers clutched everywhere, and smiles are rare. Nonetheless, we brave the frosty reception, because Lino, the federal police's river guide, lives here. He doesn't invite us into his house but promises to let us know, via "Ham-and-cheese," if a suitable canoe comes up for sale. Something tells me Lino is not going to break himself to help us. Luckily we track down another canoe, not through Lino, but through Joe's persistent efforts.

We have been in Cruzeiro for two weeks now, and are far behind on our schedule, hence Joe's increasing urgency. He spots a canoe in the harbor; half submerged and tied up to one of the Batelóns.

Eventually, Joe finds the owner and negotiates the sale: US$30. The hull is made out of a hollowed tree trunk, nearly five meters long. Thin pieces of wood attached to the sides give it a more rounded appearance. Specks of white and orange paint reveal that it had once upon a time been covered with paint.

The "new" canoe is also considerably smaller than the first one. Even with only one person and no baggage, the canoe sinks dangerously low into the water. We will not be able to take many supplies, we conclude. The supermarket is just around the corner from our hotel, and we set off to buy our supplies for the trip: 8 X Tins corned meat , 7 X Tins beef in gravy, 8 X Tins sardines , 6 X Tins Vienna Sausages, 7 X Tins tuna , 2 X Tins tomato puree, 1 kg Beans , 2 kg Rice, 4 kg Sugar , 4 kg Flour , ½ kg Coffee, Yeast, Onions, Garlic , Plastic lighters & toilet paper. As luxuries, we buy a bottle of Nautilus Cognac, peppermint sweets for Joe and cigarettes for me. But no ice cream...

Chapter 14

In a Leaking Canoe Down the Rio Juruá—The Most Winding River on Earth

"I think that to get under the surface and really appreciate the beauty of any country, one has to go there poor."

—Grace Moore

From its origin high in the Peruvian Cerros de Canchyuaya, the Rio Jurua (in Spanish Río Yurúa) winds its way patiently through more than 2400 kilometers of dense rainforest to its confluence with the Amazon main stream at Fonte Boa, in the Amazonas province of Brazil. Because the river drops only 453 meters in its entire length, the very gradual slope causes the river to flow at a very slow speed. The Jurua crosses the most humid and hottest part of the jungle and gently flows through one of the most remote parts of our planet.

Here and there you can find locals called "Caboclos." They are a group of mixed European and Indian ancestry living in small and primitive settlements which vary from one to a few huts on the bank of the river. They have no electricity, running water, or proper sanitation.

What they always do have is at least one dog and lots of children. It seems there is little else to do than to procreate. Food such as maize, pumpkin, manioc, and watermelons are planted on a small scale, and one can spot a few cattle here and there, kept on beaches or playas along the riverside. On very few occasions, one can also see a few

A Journey through Many Worlds

pigs and chickens. Fishing remains the greatest source of protein, and all the locals are in possession of nets for this purpose.

Life along the Jurua, as in many other places in the Amazon, is particularly hard and unforgiving—apart from the insect plagues, the climate is just plain awful. Here distance is measured not in kilometers, but in time, and medical help can be many days or even weeks away. It is not a tourist destination, and we met none at all while on the Jurua.

Even to buy basic provisions is a nightmare. Only the handful of larger towns on the river bank has any sort of formal shop. For the days or weeks in between these towns, you are entirely reliant on river water and fishing. The locals are also highly suspicious of strangers in the area and with the exception of a few individuals; we were largely greeted with great distaste.

Typically, the children would run off into the forest as soon as we came ashore. The adults would sit outside their huts, with silent, expressionless faces, and only if they felt like it, would they talk to us or answer any basic question. As mentioned earlier, this is the arms and drug smuggling route, and countless unsolved atrocities have been committed in this river world.

On Wednesday, the 18th of September at around 12h00 we arrive by taxi at Cruzeiro harbor. With the provisions we bought its impossible to carry everything ourselves—I guess it will come to at least 130 to 150 kilograms with all our equipment!

I wait with the baggage while Joe goes to get our newly purchased canoe from its previous owner. Twenty minutes later I can spot him rowing along towards me, his huge hat marking him out. When he gets to me, we start loading the canoe, and for a moment I am convinced we are not going to have enough space.

Just before I get in, Joe tests the canoe by rowing out into the river. As he approaches the other bank, the ferry that

In a Leaking Canoe Down the Rio Juruá

is used to move vehicles across the river begins to start up without warning. My shouts are drowned out by the drone of the ferry's engines, and I watch in horror as the steel giant bears down on the small canoe. Joe puts in an Olympian rowing effort and manages to save himself and the canoe by a hair's breadth. From where I stood, it looked so close that I was convinced the ferry would hit him. As is their custom, a group of locals gathers to watch us depart, and laugh themselves silly at our overloaded canoe. They indicate to us in frantic hand signals that we will shortly sink or topple over. In the meantime, Joe is getting more and more pissed off, and I am beginning to have my doubts too about this top heavy, overloaded tree trunk.

When we finally leave at 14h00, the canoe's clearance above water level is less than a centimeter. The slightest shift in balance results in water rushing in. As if this is not bad enough, Joe unceremoniously informs me that there is a hole in the back of the canoe as well. Our pace is painfully slow: we have to stop now and again to bail out the water. Otherwise, we will surely sink.

It is a humid, hot, cloudy day, and only four kilometers from our departure point, we find a long beach on the port side. We realize that we cannot proceed any further until some repairs are made to the canoe, and we will camp here for the night. After we have unloaded everything, we drag the canoe onto the sand.

This proves to be quite an exercise as this glorified tree trunk weighs at least 100 kilograms or more. Joe starts looking for the hole while I test my new fishing equipment, without any success. The few pieces of wood we find on the beach are soaking wet, and the fire, like the fishing, is unsuccessful.

Later that evening Joe and I sit in silence in the tent and eat cheese and tomato rolls we purchased earlier the day in Cruzeiro. Each of us has our thoughts, sitting here on the border between the Acre and Amazonas province with a leaking canoe and thousands of kilometers of murky water between us and our destination. This will be the last taste of

A Journey through Many Worlds

civilization for quite a while.

As I wake up, Joe is already hard at work repairing the canoe. Now that the mud and the old rubbish are removed, several holes are visible in the hull. Using his Leatherman, Joe cuts pieces of the floor planks away to plug the holes. Silicon sealant is then applied to seal the last cracks. To make the canoe lighter, we cut the floor planks in half and then we are on our way again.

Several canoes and 'batelons' pass us on their way to Cruzeiro. A batelon' is a flat bottomed boat carrying goods or supplies of some kind. A few kilometers further we reach the town of Canutama. Joe waits for me in the canoe while I get out in search of something to drink. We are still too close to Cruzeiro to risk drinking the polluted river water. Barefoot and with rolled up jeans, I set off into the town.

There are a few tarred streets, and I pass two military police officers who stare at me with interest out of their new 4x4. Back at the canoe, Joe cannot believe his eyes when I produce a 2 liter Coke and a pizza. Home was never like this! Many times after this, when, plagued with empty stomachs, we would think back to this pizza and coke, made possible by the road link between Cruzeiro en Canutama. But it's here that the road ends.

For the first time on the Jurua, we notice a few boats, busy fishing. After paddling 20 kilometers today, we stop at a convenient camping spot on a beach with enough useable wood.

The canoe leaks considerably less than before and floats slightly higher in the water. Things are going better! As a result of our space and weight problem with the canoe, we have to ration our food and our evening meal is sharing a 300g tin of beef (which has more sauce than meat) and rice. I notice that the moon has an eerie glow about it as the insects begin feasting.

+ + + + + +

In a Leaking Canoe Down the Rio Juruá

September 20th, 2002 (Friday)

We get up early; take down the camp, and by 08h00 we are already rowing on the river. It's early, and it is already bloody hot.

While we stop on the bank to rest for a few minutes, a batelon passes by, and its wake washes over the canoe. It is totally under water: quickly we unpack the baggage, and with great difficulty, empty it before we can continue with our journey. Were we not close to the bank when this happened, it could have been a disaster.

S 7 31'48.2" W72 28'52"

A small side tributary enters the Jurua from a south western direction. We decide to explore it, but less than a kilometer in, we have to abandon the idea as the current is too strong. Our canoe and cargo weighs at least 400 kg, and to row that upstream is no joke.

S 7 31'04" W72 28'02"

A small canal flows northwards into the Jurua, near a place where a lake is situated, according to the map. We drop anchor near the mouth of the canal, and I venture out on foot to explore.

The river bank is so muddy that it is pointless to use boots or shoes, and it is easy to slide into the sludge right up to your waist.

While Joe waits in the canoe, I follow a 'foot path' along the river for about a kilometer, when I am suddenly confronted by a Caboclo armed with a 410 shotgun. For a moment I am too shocked to move.

I will never know which one of us was more taken aback, but I know that both of our faces registered the shock right through the language and cultural barrier.

Our expressions quickly change to embarrassment, and after a few seconds we greet each other, and as a result of a lack of further vocabulary, I continue on my way. He probably came down to the lake to hunt, I think, not expecting strangely

155

A Journey through Many Worlds

dressed foreigners crossing his way. A short distance later I see the lake. It has a mirror smooth surface surrounded by the greenest trees one could ever hope to see. It has to be one of the most peaceful scenes I have ever seen anywhere. Hundreds of butterflies dart around the side, and the only disturbance on the lake are fish which break the surface now and then, most likely in search of insects.

Birds provide a melody of background music, and where the canal flows from the lake, three canoes lie tied up, drifting in uniformity with the surrounds. The lake is about 800 m long and at least half as wide. Back in the canoe, I find Joe busy trying to catch fish with his spinner which he bought in Cruzeiro. We row further until 16h40 when we reach a suitable beach.

It was a long, hard day, and my neck was roasted by the sun. We set up camp, and Joe cooks us rice which we then eat with a tin of corned meat. My sleeping bag is still wet from the flooding we suffered at the hand of the passing boat, but I am so tired that it does not bother me. The full moon changes the beach into a silvery landscape as I drift off into a deep sleep.

At six o'clock we get up, and I hang my sleeping bag and Jaguarundi skin over the tent in an attempt to dry them off. The moment that the sun appears the temperature rises fast, and because we are so close to the equator, the sun rises even faster. Within an hour, everything is dry and once we have drunk some of our make-it-yourself soft drink, we pack up camp.

We depart at 09h00. We are rowing away gently as I notice that some menacing thunder clouds are gathering. The forest on the opposite side of the river starts to come alive with sounds which seem to become more frantic and louder with each passing minute. What do they know that we don't? For a moment I can't work it out, but then I see: the approaching storm breathes life into the river.

The wind causes waves to break in our direction and next thing a downpour hits us. We row as quickly as we can to the side, and I begin to put up the tent as the wind and water

In a Leaking Canoe Down the Rio Juruá

hit us. Several minutes later the storm passes as fast as it arrived and the sun shines down again, this time relentlessly on two wet photographers with their wet tent.

While we wait for the tent to dry, we explore our enforced landing beach while numerous dolphins splash around playfully in the water. Among the gray dolphins I see another species of these freshwater friends for the first time —the pink river dolphin (Inia geoffrensis), called boto in Brazil. We set off once again, and a long way further we find a suitable beach upon which to camp.

The sun has already set as Joe videos a small Nightjar on the beach while I man his spotlight. Corned meat, rice and chilli sauce is on the menu, which is partaken under a particularly yellow moon tonight. I am once again covered in insect bites and very tired. After I have doctored my feet (this morning I was stupid enough to stand on the fireplace grid which was removed only seconds before from the fire) I plot our position on the map, and by 19h30 we are asleep.

The next day we decide to stay at our camp to try and gather some photographic material of the dolphins in particular. They are very playful and unpredictable, and hence difficult to photograph. The white sand of the beaches (playas) reflect the sun with a great intensity, and during the day it is almost unbearable without some type of shelter. For this purpose, we open both ends of the tent, (for air circulation, a vital aspect!) and throw the opened sleeping bags on top for insulation.

Inside the tent, it is almost livable but because the ends are open, we are flooded with unwelcome visitors. The sand flies descend on us like the legions from hell and happily suck our blood in the relaxing atmosphere of our shelter. The black bomber flies and mosquitoes join in as well, and together they have an insect feast.

We are by now getting a bit tired of our daily diet of corned meat, and I try my hand at fishing once again. After another round of unsuccessful attempts, I take the canoe to the other side of the river, determined to catch a fish. "Did you catch anything?" asks Joe, packing away his video camera.

A Journey through Many Worlds

"Nope" I reply. "So what's on the menu tonight?" "Pizza Joe, pizza." Joe looks at me as if my humor does not appeal to him. But supper was pizza—Jurua pizza and coffee. I mixed some flour, salt and river water into a dough, flattened it and grilled it on the fire. Not too bad with an onion and corned beef topping! And Joe's reaction? "Bloody marvelous!"

Monday the 23rd of September: We are up at 06h00, and by 07h00, the sweat is already pouring off my body. By 08h10 we are on the road again, so to speak. Bird expert Joe spots something on one of the banks and stops rowing. He stares at something which I cannot see. "What's wrong," I ask. "Look over there," says Joe, pointing to some bushes on the opposite bank, "There's a suspicious looking bird." Never before on this trip have I laughed so much, despite the undignified expression on Joe's face.

I couldn't see the bird, but the picture that came to my mind was the following: A big bird in a long coat, with a black hat low over his sunglasses, peeping over a London Times towards a government building somewhere in Prague. To me, that's a suspicious looking bird.

Joe's idea of a "suspicious looking bird" is, however, something entirely different: a collared sandpiper acting strangely by running back and forth. Upon closer inspection, we find a chick which we capture on film for future generations.

At S 7022'16.9" W 72021'30.6" we come across a small stream which looks like it originates from a lake. Our map, however, shows no lake in this area, and I once again set off to investigate while Joe guards the canoe. A few hundred meters further the vague footpath ends on the shore of a lake which has been virtually covered in a type of reddish reed. Hundreds of birds fly around in circles.

Back in the canoe, I slip back into the rowing routine. The Jurua is getting wider and wider. At one place the beach resembles a miniature of the "White Cliffs of Dover"—the beach forms a bleached white run-up to vertical sandbanks about two meters high above the water level.

In a Leaking Canoe Down the Rio Juruá

Today we reached a maximum speed of 9 km/h. We are exhausted and off to another night in Paradise.

It's the 24th of September, and today I see a real Toucan in the wild for the first time in my life! This was a great achievement, marred only by the fact that this was also the first day that we saw a Caiman before he saw or became aware of us.

The other notable thing about this day was the long, dead straight, and quite a boring stretch of river about 6km long. At least for dinner, we have an incredible variation in the menu: corned beef, black lentils, and rice. Later in the evening it begins to rain and does not stop until the next morning. We pack as much as we can into the tent to try and keep it dry.

We leave just after 09h00 today. It is a cloudy day, and our maps are proving to be increasingly inaccurate. Some "Towns" like Bom Jesus (Good Jesus) that show on our map apparently do not exist. Extrema de Pixuna appears as a big town while in reality, it is no more than five huts, and no shop at all. There is increasingly little traffic on the river, and the locals eye us with even greater suspicion than ever before. Joe is not feeling very well and is struggling with diarrhea but we keep going as best we can. We have done nearly 27 kilometers today

At 13h00 we stop on a beach so that Joe can video a Sand colored Nighthawk. The bird pretends to be injured, jumping up, flying a few feet and then landing again, in an attempt to draw our attention away from its nest. The maternal instinct.

Incredible. We camp on a beach with lots of suitable firewood. Joe has the runs again, and we suspect that it is the river water. Despite this, we go and cool off in the river before dinner. Lentils, corned beef, and rice. An unnatural screeching of a group of Howler monkeys announce the dawn of a new day. Before our departure, I manage to photograph an exotic looking butterfly. The wings are pitch black, marked only by a diagonal yellow stripe and two red spots.

A Journey through Many Worlds

It looks like the weather pattern is going to change. The clouds have gathered in, and do not move the whole day. Joe still has diarrhea and is now throwing up as well. I just pray that it is not Malaria... we are far from any proper help. From the south, a river flows into the Jurua and here is a large town with about 30 houses. I plot it on the GPS: S 7° 12'43.5" W 72° 03'00.2"

Pink dolphins abound, and near the town, we see two caimans in the bush on the river bank. Even though the leaks in the canoe are still not completely sealed, our clearance above the water is now some 4 cm: an indication we are working our way through the corned meat. At the town, Joe buys sugar and a type of "cream cracker" biscuits. I am by now getting used to the rowing, and with every stroke, the oar makes two small whirlpools which suck the water with a slurping noise.

Joe says we are going too fast, but I think it is pointless to sit on the beach and burn to death. In the canoe there is airflow, and the temperature is a lot lower.

Now and then thousands of sand flies descend on the canoe, but that does not happen nearly as often as in the tent. At about 14h00, the clouds open their windows, and for 45 minutes the rain pours down, accompanied by thunder and lightning.

We stay in the canoe, and my poncho does not pass the Amazon test. It leaks particularly badly in a critical area; around the neck. As the storm passes, we see a large flock of green Lauritas, a small parrot, fly past, screeching noisily. I can't help but wonder what they taste like.

When we have eaten our sardines on rice and gulped down our coffee, it is dark, and we take the canoe to the other side of the river. Here we have seen reptile eyes flashing in the spotlight, and Joe hopes to capture something on video.

Whatever it was, it is too clever for us and disappears into the water before we are even close. We could not even determine its size. Just before we get into the tent, there is a hell of a splash in the water alongside the canoe. The

In a Leaking Canoe Down the Rio Juruá

waves flood the canoe, and the ripples are visible spreading across the river. Almost out of respect, Joe, I and the jungle are quiet for a few moments.

Then a frog croak breaks the silence, and the nightlife starts up again as if nothing has happened.

"Was that a ...dolphin, Joe?" I ask.

"No, the water is too shallow there—probably an alligator or caiman that caught something" Joe replies nonchalantly. By this time, however, we have had it with our limited menu, and that caiman had better watch his step near us. However, we rowed 24.1 km today, and I am too tired to even dream of alligators or other jungle nasties.

+ + + + + +

September 27th, 2002 (Friday)

It has been raining from early this morning, and we decide to stay home today. To pack up in the rain is a disaster and we can do with a day's rest. The whole day is cloudy, yet still, the sand is boiling hot. We have peas, onions, fish, and rice.

The mosquitoes drive you mad and at 18h00, like clockwork they attack. If you get into the tent, a batch always follows you, and you spend the next half hour trying to kill the intruders. For some reason, they appear not to be so interested in Joe, but I am absolutely sick and tired of them! When all the insects and I finally come to rest, I lie and listen to the nighttime noises, and the alligators catching fish outside the tent: Snap. Splash!

+ + + + + +

September 28th, 2002 (Saturday)

We leave at 07h45 under a thick cloud cover and row 33.7 km, the furthest in any one day yet, at an average speed of 4.8 km/h. Joe still spots "suspicious looking birds" here, there and everywhere, much to my amusement. At about 15h00 we land to search for a Tern nest.

A thunderstorm breaks out, and we sit in the canoe for an hour waiting for it to pass. As soon as it is over, you see

161

A Journey through Many Worlds

the Collared Plovers running around on the beaches looking for insects that have been driven to the surface of the sand by the water. We find a suitable camp spot at 17h30, and we empty the sopping canoe once again. Joe somehow gets a fire going with some wet wood, and we have an incredible dinner of corned beef, lentils and rice. After gazing at a glorious sunset, we go to sleep.

+ + + + + +

September 29th, 2002 (Sunday).

Tomorrow we should be at Ipixuna where we can re-supply ourselves, but I cannot but wonder how big the place will be. It seems as if the further we row, the more rain falls. We get at least one storm per day, and often more. I am now used to sleeping in a wet sleeping bag, funny how you can get accustomed to anything. I roll the film container in my sleeping bag during the day for insulation against the temperature. This is placed inside my Busby suitcase, but during the storms and resultant waves on the river, the water still gets in and makes everything wet. The bag rests on the sides of the canoe, but that does not help matters at all because sometimes there is so much water inside the canoe that the bottom of the case is immersed in it. If only I could get hold of some plastic, then I would be able again to enjoy a dry nights sleep.

After today's storm, I found some maize and pumpkin growing on one of the beaches (amazing), and we eat this unexpected bonus with corned meat and rice.

+ + + + + +

September 30th, 2002 (Monday)

24 Kilometers of rowing and plenty pink dolphins later a big town appears on the northern bank of the Jurua. It must be Ipixuna at last!! Less than 500 meters from the town an enormous thunderstorm breaks out, and we have to reroute to the safety of the nearest playa.

Half an hour later we dock our tree trunk next to a canoe that looks even worse than ours. "Stallone II" announces its

In a Leaking Canoe Down the Rio Juruá

name in big red letters on the side. According to our maps, this will be the last big town for several hundred kilometers, so it will be wise to use the opportunity to freshen up and replenish our supplies.

I wait in the canoe while Joe tries to find transport and safe accommodation for us and our canoe. Ipixuna is a weird place. After nearly two weeks of jungle and brown river water, we are walking on tarred roads in the middle of the Amazon! The roads are for internal traffic only as the town is not connected to any other destination by road.

Your only travel options from here are via the river or the local airfield.

Our first "civilized" meal in a while consists of beef, beans, spaghetti and salad—all for a mere R$4! The bad thing about pitching up in a remote jungle town with a fucked up canoe and looking like Indiana Jones on a bad day is finding accommodation...

The locals are watching us from a distance with expressions saying "These gringos are baaaad news for this town."

At the first two local "hotels" Joe is bluntly informed that there are no rooms available. The third one, hotel "Yanne" with its two floors is probably the newest skyscraper in this part of the rainforest.

The owner seems desperate (or maybe nervous is a better word) enough to let the two dirty strangers in at R$22 per head. And we are desperate and tired enough to accept the over inflated price. The small air conditioned room is tiled, and in one corner there is an 80L Consul fridge. The best part is it's filled with beer, mineral water, and soft drinks.

In the opposite corner, there is a color TV, and the entrance next to it leads to a lovely clean shower, complete with fresh towels. Nothing can beat this after a tough day at the office! Well, maybe one more thing, but that would be pushing it.

Outside the sounds of the Brazilian presidential elections are echoing in the streets. Unreal to think of the impact of

163

A Journey through Many Worlds

it even here in the jungle. Fire crackers are exploding while lies are being broadcasted over portable speakers and I drift away peacefully to a dreamland in my soft and dry Amazon bed.

+ + + + + +

October 1st, 2002 (Tuesday)

Our breakfast ensures that we have to stay another day in Ipixuna. The pawpaw, scrambled eggs, bread and milky coffee, was too much for our frail stomachs to tolerate. Most of the day we spent inside the hotel—either in the bathroom or sorting out and cleaning our kit and equipment.

If we feel better, we intend to leave tomorrow after buying some more supplies.

+ + + + + +

October 2nd, 2002 (Wednesday)

5 X tins corned meat, 5 X tins beef in gravy, 5 X tins sardines , 4 X tins viennas , 4 kg sugar , 4 kg flour .

We could at least survive another month or more on that!

The taxi back to the riverbank and the storage fee of the canoe is R$20, and at around 09h20 we depart. 8 Kilometers further we stop and pitch camp. It's a lovely spot with pumpkin growing on the beach which we incorporate in our corned beef, beans and rice supper. After a nice swim and wash in the river, I enter the tent to get my map work up to date. After killing 31 mosquitos, I go to sleep. I know it's a bad sign... I started counting them...

October 3rd, 2002 (Thursday)

Yet another thunderstorm and accompanying waves force us to the shore and while we wait for it to pass I notice a gray dolphin darting several times teasingly into mid air with a fish in its mouth. By late afternoon we stop just in time to put up camp. From 4 different directions, I see the dark clouds of approaching storms.

The scene that follows is an amazing high voltage aerial display with blue lightning bolts shooting horizontally across

164

In a Leaking Canoe Down the Rio Juruá

the sky while the thunder shakes the earth. It's clear that we are entering a wetter part of our journey.

+ + + + + +

October 4th, 2002 (Friday)

I awake with the sounds of "Happy birthday". Did Joe totally lose it? Maybe he has Malaria after all, and now he's becoming delirious. No, maybe I lost it I realize as I check the date. Shit. It's my birthday, and I forgot about it! I knew it was coming up, but I totally lost track of time. Not even last night, as I was writing in my diary, did I realize it. It's a bad sign, Johan, a bad sign.

We measure the width of the river with the GPS—137 meters, and at 14h00 we row into another tropical storm. This one is not so bad as it's not hitting us directly and we decide to keep rowing. There are dolphins everywhere, and at 15h00 we spot something suspicious on the beach. This time it's not a bird but the remains of a big black caiman. Today is also the birthday of my friend Bernice, and she made me promise to bring her a tooth from the Amazon— preferably not an Indian tooth she explained, but one from some exotic animal.

My loyal Leatherman did the job and in no time, plenty sand fly bites and 4 (alligator) teeth later I am back in the canoe, and we're off. We don't manage to dry out before yet another storm hits us at 16h30. Shit! That's enough for one day.

At the jungle side of the beach, a few overhanging trees form a kind of protective canopy, and we pitch the tent. This is the first beach we come across that would be suitable for camping in the daytime too because of the trees, and we decide to take a break for a few days here. It will also give us the opportunity to explore a bit without rushing it.

Joe prepares supper and afterward hands me a handwritten birthday card addressed to 'My Best Travel

165

A Journey through Many Worlds

Companion.' I guess I must be yes... also his only travel companion! It's time for the festivities to begin! From somewhere Joe produces a large tin of 'Goiabada'—some kind of guava marmalade that's enjoyed together with cheese as a dessert.

Interestingly the word 'marmalade' originated from the Portuguese 'marmalade'—preserved quince (Portuguese—marmelo) used as rations on galleons many moons ago. Here in Brazil, the Portuguese substituted the quince for guavas.

In my backpack, I find what is left of the Nautilus Cognac that we bought earlier. We sit back and enjoy our unlikely Amazon sundowners and dessert until the first mosquitos arrive.

But somehow I don't mind them so much tonight. The thought of spending your birthday here, sipping cheap Cognac instead of river water and knowing tomorrow you can sleep late is amazing.

Well... it's difficult to explain. Maybe the jungle has got the better of me already! Our Position is S 6° 59' 27.8" W 71°26' 27.6"

+ + + + + +

October 5th, 2002 (Saturday)

We wake at 5h40 with the sound of hundreds of parakeets feasting on an eroded clay overhang against the opposite riverbank. This is called a 'clay lick,' and it is believed that parrots and macaws eat the clay that acts as an antidote against some toxins they may consume as part of their diet. You can call it a kind of a Parrot Rennie.

This is a rare sight in the wild, and we mobilize our canoe as fast as possible. Unfortunately, the birds disperse as soon as we are nearly close enough to photograph them. SHIT!!!

We shall definitely have to stay here and get some video and pictures. We move our tent to get maximum shadow time from the overhanging trees. Above the tent, I put up our ground sail which we generally use to cover the equipment in the canoe. This together with the tent forms a double ceiling

166

In a Leaking Canoe Down the Rio Juruá

against the sun, while not obstructing airflow.

In the meantime, Joe has left for the opposite bank where he plans to put up two camouflaged hides from where he will try and photograph the birds. As I look towards where Joe was minutes before, I see only the vegetation and clay face of the river bank. Joe has become part of his environment with the skill of a seasoned commando. I am amazed at the competence and patience of this man. Later Joe returns and we go about normal camp routine.

Delta wing black flies attack my arms and face as I try to knead dough for some bread tonight. Why is nothing easy in this bloody place? Joe returns, and we try to fix the small solar panel for AA batteries.

A few lone cattle come walking from the opposite side of the beach towards our camp. They must belong to one of the local farmers on the riverbank. I still imagine a sizzling medium rare rump steak when all of a sudden Joe gives a cry like a Viking on Ecstasy, grabs a machete and storms the enemy, gaze fixed on the closest target.

What the fuck?? Did Joe go totally nuts? Something has triggered this quiet, composed introvert.

The terrified cow accelerated at an un-cowly speed and was it not for the huge beach I would probably have had my steak. Joe sees he is going to lose this race and throws the machete at the animal, using it as a giant dart. He misses, and suddenly I realize I am not hungry anymore. I am worried. Very worried.

"You want to talk about it Joe?"

"Bloody Bovine Bastards....God, they are stupid."

Then, after a few moments of silence, Joe shares his feelings with me. Many years ago, Joe explained, he was photographing some kind of rare bird.

With his incredible patience, he waited for days and days for the eggs to hatch. Then all of a sudden the camera viewfinder was filled with a few hundred pounds of a pure bloody bovine bastard. A cow decided the nest would make

A Journey through Many Worlds

a lovely resting place! Joe describes this as "Fucked by the fickle finger of fate."

My dear friend, I understand!

At around 13h00 about 40 parrots return to the bank. They have fantastic colors—some are green with blue heads and red tails. A bright green Iguana visits our tent to have a look at this alien party.

It's clear that the climate is changing, or rather that we have moved into a new climatic zone. Every day we have thunderstorms now. Sitting in a canoe on this huge river and hitting a tropical storm is something impossible to explain.

It is now 15h00, and although it feels much warmer, my thermometer measures 28°C in the shade. The humidity must be far over 90%, and that will explain the unbearable perception of heat. The temperature of the river is the same— also 28°C.

After a search for good wood, we make a fire, and I break the dough I made earlier into smaller portions. When the last flames are gone, I put it on the cooking grid and then sit back to enjoy the magic moments before mosquito time at 18h00. We enjoy the bread together with some tinned beef cubes and lentils before entering the tent for some rest.

+ + + + + +

October 6th, 2002 (Sunday)

This morning I try again to charge my AA batteries— without success. I take Joe with the canoe to the opposite bank so that he can take up position in one of the hides before the parrots arrive for their clay meal. He will spend the day there in his hide with the video camera.

At the campsite, I am visited by more green lizards, and I watch as they lick the dew from the grass and plants. The biggest of these lizards I estimate at around 70 cm in length.

As I observe them, their diet appears to be mostly roots and grass. I also observe a spotted tody-flycatcher (Todirostrum Maculatum). These insectivores hunt in pairs and alone

168

In a Leaking Canoe Down the Rio Juruá

from sea level and up to 500 meters.

The temperature is around 30°C, and later in the afternoon I take the canoe to pick up Joe from his hide. I hope he got some great footage!

Tonight we will have another "bully beef and rice" session.

It's the 7th of October and we get up early at 05h30. Today I will do the hide session, and Joe takes me to the hide across the river while I am rethinking the logic of volunteering to do this for the chance to get a photo of a bird eating clay.

Sitting with minimum to no movement for a long period awaiting your subject to appear can be extremely mind-numbing. Especially if the thought of lighting a cigarette and enjoying a relaxing walk on the river bank while observing the amazing nature, bird and insect life pops up from time to time.

My eye caught some movement to my right and combined with the sound of moving water I turn my head while keeping the camera in position. Then I spot the head of a large black caiman, around 4 meters long, as it swims a mere 3 meters away from my position towards the bank. It moves out of my angle of view, and I once again think of how observant one has to be in the wild. I did not spot it before it moved. When I was in the military many years ago, I was taught about the five "S's and an M" in camouflage. Some of the things that can compromise your position are "Shape, Shine, Shadow, Silhouette, Spacing and Movement." Here it was the "M" that alerted me at first.

Moments later it begins to rain and while I am getting drenched, I observe two pink dolphins in the direction of our camping site across the river. Suddenly a wasp attacks my arm and rips me back into the Amazon reality. It's about 14h00, and I think I have done my part in this attempted photography session. The score of Wasp—1, Caiman—0 and Johan—0 is perfectly fine for me thanks.

Time to go back home, to the tent I mean.

Joe arrives with the canoe and we return to the opposite

169

A Journey through Many Worlds

bank. I fetch my line and hooks and start to prepare for fishing. It does not take too long to land three medium sized catfish. This combined with lentils is a great meal, and it brings my total number of fishes caught to a round 30. Time for a rest after an exciting day.

+ + + + + +

October 8th, 2002 (Tuesday)

It's Joe's turn again for using the hide and I take him to the opposite bank with the canoe. It's not a good photo day and after fetching him again, I fish. It's amazing how well dough mixed with beef stock attracts the fishes! I land a fat catfish of about 45cm and roast it the evening over our little grid.

After this, we sharpen the machetes again on the stone we brought.

+ + + + + +

October 9th, 2002 (Wednesday)

Same place. Last night it started raining, and it continued for 12 hours up to 06h00 this morning. I must say, the tent is doing a great job so far. It's keeping us dry, and it also does an excellent job in keeping any stray mosquitos inside. With the latest fish, I caught today it brings the total number to 32. The fish is not that big, but it can be a good starter meal. Joe is back in the hide but not so lucky today; he does not get any real good footage.

Next, a canoe with some locals (Caboclos) arrives. The communication gap is a bit big, and after a long conversation which is not understood by any of the parties, I indicate with "Amanja" and enthusiastic hand signals that we will be leaving the area tomorrow. Just in case they thought we wanted to retire here or something.

+ + + + + +

October 10th 2002 (Thursday)

Starting at 07h30 this morning, we paddled 30.3

In a Leaking Canoe Down the Rio Juruá

kilometers today—6 hours moving at an average of 5 km/h. By 12h00 we have already done 20 km. I'm not feeling well this evening. I have no appetite and no energy. We have to eat so we bake some bread. In the morning we can see (measured against the stick that anchors our canoe) that the water level has risen by at least 30 centimeters after the rain.

Our tent looks like a 'little house of horrors' with all the blood stripes and spots of all the squashed mosquitos so far.

As I step outside, I see several caiman tracks between our tent and the canoe. It's early and we should get going.

+ + + + + +

October 11th 2002 (Friday)

S 6° 57' 13.9" W 71° 13' 18.5". 33.4km 4.7km/h average.

It's extremely hot and we manage to pitch the tent only moments before it starts raining. Our meal is only half a tin of corned meat each. After the rain has stopped, we manage to get some sugar in a small village on the opposite bank of the river. Finishing our meal in silence, Joe suddenly say: "You know what Johan, I really think we should go camping sometime!" Well, I don't know what to say. With all the moisture and water my feet are getting sores, and it's tough to stay dry.

+ + + + + +

October 12th 2002 (Saturday)

S 6° 53' 27.1" W 71° 7' 15.4".

We did 41.4 km today at 4.7km/h average 8hours, 42minutes. Today was the longest day yet. Dead tired—we spent nearly 10 hours in the canoe and had two tins of beef cubes, our last ration of spaghetti and tomato puree—what a fantastic meal it was.

What I suspect was a dolphin quickly surfaced about 50 cm from me next to the canoe and then disappears again. It happened twice, and I can't believe missing it both times. Joe also did not get a proper look to determine what it was. According to my map, we are now close to another Indigenous

171

A Journey through Many Worlds

area that borders on the river. After setting up camp, we fall asleep with the sound of an Amazon thunderstorm.

+ + + + + +

October 13th 2002 (Sunday)

S 6° 49' 57.6" W 71° 0' 34.3". 33.6km 4.6km/h average 7hours 16minutes.

Another hot day—I can feel my skin burning, and I put on some ointment. On my map, a place called 'Recife' is indicated, but in our real world, it is not visible. We are very, very tired, and our food supply is dwindling. We are out of sugar again, so it's only Bully beef and peas on the menu tonight.

+ + + + + +

October 14th 2002 (Monday)

S 6° 46' 35.9" W 70° 52' 6.3". 27.3km 4.5km/h average 6hours 40minutes.

I photographed a caiman again today. Well, the caiman belongs to the same family as alligators, namely Alligatoridae. These two species are more related to each other than the crocodile which belongs to the Crocodylidae family. I see a smaller caiman, paroling around a bigger one not far from us.

It's a real big caiman, and I suspect it's a male. On the bank of the river, we observe a neat house. Not one of the typical wooden shack houses you find from time to time, but a very neat one.

We stop, and we are greeted by the owner and local farmer, Zhay Cordiera. He is a very pleasant man with an open face. On the porch in front of the house are several large white and blue pots containing plants. He invites us into his home and ask us very politely to please eat something. I guess we must look hungry...

His wife appears and puts fish, beef, yuca and fried eggs in front of us!! What an amazing gift from above!! As we enjoy the most fantastic out-of-the-blue meal, I think about Life

In a Leaking Canoe Down the Rio Juruá

and how sometimes good things can happen so unexpectedly. Against the walls, I observe an extensive collection of shiny aluminum pots of different sizes.

Zhay has six children. First, he says five, but then he says no, he forgot about one. It's actually six. He is very inquisitive and asks many questions. He wants to know what we eat on the river, do we drink the river water, how and where we camp and many other things.

"Cuidado com Jacare!!" Beware of the alligators! He warns us—they are very dangerous! This man is not your average river farmer. He has a television and parabolic dish antenna. Wow, this was so unexpected, and it broke the routine that was set for so many days.

After greeting our new friends, we are off paddling downstream until we find a nice spot to camp on a river beach. Luckily we could buy 4 kg of sugar from Zhay and we enjoy a steaming cup of coffee before I photograph a spectacular sunset. We don't need to eat tonight—all the food today, wow!

Shining the spotlight from the tent we can see three sets of caiman eyes reflecting back red. I think about the warning Zhay made and wonder how they would respond if we move closer. We carefully walk closer only to see them slip into the water again with a splash. One cannot see the physical size in the darkness, only the eyes. Maybe we can get a better idea tomorrow if we see their tracks. It's quiet, and I can't sleep, so I take my handline and try to fish but then the silence is broken by some cattle that we hear as they are walking towards our camp site. "God, they are stupid, bloody bovine bastards" I hear Joe mumbling in the tent. I catch no fish tonight, and it's around 23h00 that I go to sleep feeling a little hungry for the first time since that meal at Zhay's.

+ + + + + +

October 15th 2002 (Tuesday)

S 6° 47' 50" W 70° 43' 39.5".

Today we did 37.1km at 4.4km/h average 8hours

A Journey through Many Worlds

27minutes moving. It's a real shitty morning, and everything is wet. The canoe is full of water, and my boots are wet. Depressing. The wind is blowing, and it causes some waves on the water. Because the water clearance of the canoe is very small, the waves cause the canoe to catch water and it also seems to be leaking quite a bit! Soon our feet are covered in water, but we push on.

A school of five pink Amazon river dolphins (Inia Geoffrensis), also known as boto or bufeo has been following us for several kilometers. I know it's the same ones because I can identify one with a unique scar on the right side. The pink river dolphin is the largest species of river dolphin and can reach over 180kg (40lb) in weight, and they can feed on more than 50 species of fish, including the piranha.

Around lunchtime, we stop and enjoy a bully beef lunch on the river bank. For sure NOT the best lunch because of all the little flies and other small flying monsters. By around 17h00 we identify a beautiful beach with enough wood, no cattle and not too many mosquitoes!

I am using the GPS now directly on the 12V battery because the solar panel is not operating due to the cloud cover. And the cloud cover is 100% for the last several hours. Beef and peas on rice tonight.

Because the mosquitos are giving us a break this evening, we are allowed to sit chatting next to the campfire until 21h30.

+ + + + + +

October 16th 2002 (Wednesday)

S 6° 48' 25.7" W 70° 46' 06.2". 7.1km 3.2km/h 2hours 14minutes.

We paddle up the Rio Gregorio. On the map, it looks like we are again in an indigenous area. We observe many caimans here, and we decide to find a camping place between the trees that are sticking out of the water in order not to attract attention from any people unnecessarily.

First I have difficulty to catch a fish here, but when I

In a Leaking Canoe Down the Rio Juruá

eventually got one, I cut it up for bait and moved to another spot nearby.

This was a good idea because as my hook with bait touched the water, the whole area around it came alive with movement. Catfish.

Within seconds I catch a piranha, and I use the leatherman to remove the hook and then throw the fish in a bucket. I repeat the process, and within 20 minutes I caught eleven piranhas and one catfish. I am sure this will be our biggest meal in ages, and I drop my Leatherman, drenched in Piranha blood, into a tree root that emerges from the ground.

After we enjoyed our piranha food festival, I will retrieve the trustworthy Leatherman and clean it properly. I am looking around the camp area for signs of former habitation and find what appears to be an old piece of carved but severely eroded wood.

Possibly it was washed down during one of the previous wet seasons, or maybe it has been laying here for a long time? I wish I knew what it was or to whom it belonged.

We are in a very secluded area now and out of direct sunlight. We pitch our hammocks between some of the smaller trees and take a little rest in the late afternoon. Luckily there are not too many insects here, and we enjoy the special time. I think of all the caiman we saw on the way up this stream.

The birdlife and forest coverage here is also much denser and visible than on the Jurua main stream. One of the birds that I see for the first time in my life that really fascinates me is the Hoatzin (Opisthocomus Hoazin). Some people call this tropical bird the "stinkbird" and it is found in different parts of the Amazon and Orinoco Delta in South America.

Its name derives from its unpleasant manure-like odor which is a result of the bacterial fermentation of the leaves they eat.

+ + + + + +

A Journey through Many Worlds

October 17th 2002 (Thursday)

S 6° 48' 14.0" W 70° 40' 44.8" 22.7km 4.2km/h average 5hours 22minutes.

We leave early, pack up and go down the stream and turn right onto the Jurua mainstream again. Then I get a shock—I must have left my Leatherman at the camp!!! I still remember catching all the fish and using the Leatherman to remove the hooks from the Piranhas mouths. The Leatherman is absolutely a "must have" for somebody new in this world of sharp tooth fish.

Unfortunately, it will not be easy to turn around with our bulky tree trunk of a canoe and navigate back up the Jurua for several kilometers to backtrack our route and find the Leatherman. Damn!

In a short period I count seven caimans, and after we anchor our canoe near the bank of the river, we bake bread and only leave camp again at around 12h00. It is overcast today, and when we reach a river beach that looks okay, we anchor the canoe again.

The water's visibility on the Jurua is about 30cm today, and I remember it was much less in the murky waters of the Rio Gregorio. Joe starts the fire with cow (bovine bastard) dung. He did not do it to be creative, but there were no useful pieces of wood or branches to be found.

Today we will bake bread on a cow dung fire and enjoy it with beef cubes and rice. Joe talks a bit about his travels and adventures in Japan and Australia and we are off to bed early.

+ + + + + +

October 18th 2002 (Friday)

S 6° 49' 11" W 70° 32' 28.4" 34.9 km 7hours 39minutes moving.

Today we are one month out of Cruzeiro do Sul! The day starts with an early tropical rain shower at 06h00 which is followed by a surrealistic Howler Monkey choir that emerge

In a Leaking Canoe Down the Rio Juruá

unseen from the dense tree and foliage wall not far from the river bank.

For dinner, we have bully beef and peas which we enjoy while watching the incredible sunset in the West.

We observe many caimans on the bank of the river and go to bath in the shallow water while keeping our watchful eyes wide open.

++++++

October 19th 2002 (Saturday)

S 6° 45' 25.6" W 70° 24' 20.2". 52.4km, 5km/h average 10hours 30minutes moving.

It was a long day. Today a small fish jumped out of the water and into the canoe, right between my bare feet. For a fraction of a second, I thought it was a piranha and nearly jumped into the water. Stupid moment of the day, but luckily for me it was just an innocent little fish with a good sense of humor. We are very tired and open our last tin of beans for dinner which we only finish at 22h00.

The location indicated as "Uniao" on the map was nowhere to be seen today.

My feet are sore, and by tomorrow we will run out of coffee, and I will be out of tobacco. It is full moon tonight, and we only stopped paddling around 19h00.

Magical landscape with not too many mosquitos tonight. I fall asleep after along day and dream of eating ham...

++++++

20 October 2002 (Sunday)

S 6° 43' 44.3" W 70° 18' 26.2". 31km at 5km/h average 6hours 11minutes.

We sleep late. After waking up, we enjoy a morning coffee while looking at a spectacular gray dolphin river show.

They are playing and enjoying themselves in the river in front of us, and you can almost think they're enjoying the audience. The next moment one of the dolphins suddenly

A Journey through Many Worlds

darts several feet straight up out of the water before it turns and disappears back in the golden brown water of the Jurua. These creatures are very difficult to photograph because they don't usually surface at a predictable location.

We continue our canoe voyage downstream, and at one stage a motorized canoe comes up from behind. The skipper is a friendly half-Indian, and he offers to tow our canoe behind his.

It is a kind offer that we don't accept, and we continue until we reach a small community in the middle of nowhere. It is marked as "Comunidad Deixa Falar."

Joe stays with the canoe while I climb the river bank to see what provisions I can find. A short while later I return with 4 x tins of meatloaf, some condensed milk, soy oil and tobacco for my pipe—all for R$ 17. I also see some toys in the form of logging trucks. Kids from a small age will get accustomed to logging—I guess that's the idea?

After we continue paddling, it starts to rain, but we just keep going. The river transport is getting busier, and at one point we are nearly hit by a passing barge. Luckily we can get out of the way in time. You can misjudge yourself with the speed and size of some of these river vessels! Another playful dolphin pushes lightly against our canoe and the next moment teasingly grabs Joe's paddle. This kind of contact with the creatures of the wild is very special.

Not long after, we find a beach to camp for the night and follow the normal procedure—I pitch the tent while Joe starts to find wood for the fire. An Indian canoe appears with family onboard, and they stop close to us. I observe them and wonder what their intentions are. Normally the locals and Indians will just ignore us or view us cautiously from a distance. But not this family.

I am standing next to my camera that's mounted on the tripod, busy setting up for some sunset photos. First, the Indians walk to Joe and observe the strange green object that we call a dome tent.

They seem to be fascinated by it, and once they are

178

In a Leaking Canoe Down the Rio Juruá

finished walking around and touching the flexible structure they walk towards me with eyes and frowns that say "what the hell is this?"

No aggression, just innocent childish curiosity. One of the Indians, an older woman, remained in the canoe. I turn my telephoto zoom lens towards her and change the focal length to 500 to get a nice closeup image of her looking through squinting eyes towards me. Then I show one of the curious bystanders with hand signals to look through the camera eyepiece. The Indian with the red striped face utters a sudden gasp that's combined with a strange but loud sound.

To me, it sounded somehow like I imagine a howler monkey's first unexpected encounter with King Kong would sound. Then he turns his puzzled face in my direction with an expression that yelled in all earthly languages—how do you do this magic?? Now how do you explain this, without any knowledge of his mother tongue, to somebody who has obviously never seen a lens or any other optical instrument?

I don't know. All I did was to show all the Indians while the lady sitting in the canoe was obviously getting irritated by this strange behavior of everybody on the bank. One of the Indian women standing about a meter and a half from me then suddenly crouches.

I look down amazed at her strange behavior. A moment later I observe the sand close to her feet changing color. This woman is pissing next to me while I try to photograph a spectacular Amazon sunset. The other Indians are just looking at my camera, and this behavior is apparently quite normal. To each his own. Maybe 10 minutes later the family is on their way home with the canoe, and we can relax and talk about another exciting day in South America. Tonight we have a lot of mosquitos again.

For food, we have meatloaf, pumpkin, and rice and there is a definite drop in temperature by 19h00. Time to put on a jacket and not long after that its time for bed.

+ + + + + +

A Journey through Many Worlds

October 21st 2002 (Monday)

S 6° 44' 47.8" W 70° 12' 31.2". 40.3km 4.4km/h 9hours 4minutes

Today we saw a big thunderstorm approaching. The map is not accurate and the place "San José" is marked totally wrong. On the way, we eat the watermelon that we harvested on one of the beaches.

When we arrived at a good camping spot I count the most mosquitos ever gathering on my ankle, and I quickly count between 40-50 of them, trying to drain me from various angles. The bad news is that our Repelex anti-insect lotion is nearly finished, but I believe there must still be "Bushman" insect repellent left. This stuff is the best, and it is water resistant. I always like to keep at least one of the tubes of Bushman gel in 'reserve.'

Tonight we will enjoy the last meatloaf and rice. We must make a plan to get food replenishments by tomorrow.

+ + + + + +

October 22nd 2002 (Tuesday)

S 6° 43' 03.0" W 70° 7' 18.5". 37.5km 4km/h 9hhours 15minutes moving.

According to the Garmin, it is 29 kilometers as the macaw flies to the next, large town before we reach the main stream. The town is called Eirunepe.

Before we reach our camp for the evening, we encounter another canoe with locals, and they sell us some eggs for R$1. We fry the eggs and bully beef and enjoy a super meal. It was a terribly hot day and as the sun sets we are engulfed by a terrible wave of mosquito arriving at 18h00 sharp. This was the biggest mozzie attack yet, and the tent zip is starting to give problems—it doesn't want to "lock" properly, and the tent is FULL of mosquitoes!

+ + + + + +

October 23rd 2002 (Wednesday)

S 6° 44' 47.2" W 70° 0' 54.9". 28.5km 5km/h 5hours

In a Leaking Canoe Down the Rio Juruá

44minutes moving.

We only leave at around 10h30, and it has been raining the whole morning. I have diarrhea and feel terrible. We are paddling in the rain, and the sand flies cover us like a black mist. These tiny little fuckers can cause many problems including leishmaniasis that can manifest in the form of variously terrible ulcers on the skin, mouth and/or nose as well as fever, low red blood cells, and enlarged liver. Leishmaniasis kills tens of thousands of people yearly all around the world. It is the female sand fly which transmits the protozoa, Leishmania. To escape the hordes of sand flies we make an early strategic retreat to our tent at 16h45 and pretend to enjoy some cold bully beef.

++++++

October 24th 2002 (Thursday)

S 6° 41' 33.2" W 69° 54' 34.4" 51.8km 5.2 average ± 9hours 10minutes.

Today we have an early start and start paddling at 06h40. Because of the dense cloud cover, our solar panel doesn't charge the battery, and we loose GPS signal. But luckily there is no rain today.

On the beach, we see a cat and dog, so there must be some civilization around. Not much further we encounter a local half-Indian in a canoe. The friendly man offers us a peace token in the form of a watermelon. This is a token which we gladly accept!

With our limited vocabulary, we understand that it is still about 16 days of paddling to reach Manaus, the capital of the Amazonas province.

On the beach where we set up camp, we meet some more friendly locals, and they offer us a place to sleep in a structure also used as a school. The insect and sand fly swarms are massive here, and we have to use our Bushman repellant. I take some video footage of Joe while he is paddling on the river.

Dinner will be only rice and chilli sauce because there is

A Journey through Many Worlds

no meat left. Again we make an early retreat to the tent after we saw the approach of a wave of moths and insects.

$$+ + + + + +$$

October 25th, 2002 (Friday)

After we put the sponsor sticker of Agfa and Leatherman on the canoe, I tie the canoe to a stick in the shallow water. Joe gets in while I set up my tripod and the Pentax K1000 camera. There is a 50mm lens mounted on the camera and I pre-focus on the front section of the canoe. Next, I set the manual timer to a 10-second delay, press the shutter release and jump into the canoe with my paddle in hand. I repeat this three times to make sure we can get something for the sponsors.

We depart at around 08h30 and paddle the 6.4 kilometers to Eirunepe. In the distance, I can see a huge radio antenna and around 40 vultures circling up front. It's only a little more than an hour later that I can see a big three deck vessel in the harbor and I wonder if it will leave in the direction of Manaus in the next few days.

As we are docking, three military policemen arrive and request that one of us must accompany them to the station for a "conversação" (conversation). The locals are all staring at these strangers as I follow the police up the road to the station. In front of the station, there are vehicles parked. They are neatly marked "Policia Militar." As I enter the office, the police chief behind the desk introduces himself as "Ten." After introducing myself, I hand over the report of the Federal Police in Cruzeiro do Sul as well as our passports. After a minute he looks up suddenly, and with a piercing light brown eyes he asks "ARMAS?"

From my days in the South African Army in Angola as well as later with Executive Outcomes in Angola I build up a small but useful little Portuguese vocabulary for basic war zone survival. "Nao Armas, Capitan—Nao Problema." After I show him our intended route on a map in his office, he copies the Federal Police report without reading it.

Then Captain Ten indicates that he wants to inspect our

In a Leaking Canoe Down the Rio Juruá

canoe. We don't have any choice, and we accompany them back to where Joe is waiting at the canoe. As they are doing a quick but detailed spot check of out kit and equipment, I take my camera to photograph the latest moment of our adventure.

The next moment one of the policeman jumps forward with open hands held in front of the camera lens and the volume of his verbal protest is rising to uncomfortable levels. Mental note: Do not attempt to photograph the Brazilian Military Police when they are on duty.

When nothing illegal is found, they chat to us and ask detail about our trip and where we started, etc. "Con remo??"—By rowing?? they ask and immediately think we are crazy to do this. We absolutely agree, and when they leave, Joe starts to look for a local passenger boat to take us to Manaus on the Amazon main stream.

It doesn't take long for Joe to confirm that the wisest choice would be to take the "Rei Saul" to Manaus. The crew of the big green and white three deck vessel is very accommodating, and they invite us to stay on board although the boat is only leaving on Monday.

We put all our kit on the second deck and put our hammocks up. It is clear that the Roman Catholic culture is having a strong influence even here, deep in the Brazilian Rainforest. There are two signs on the open deck that indicate that ladies and gentlemen must sleep in two different (open) sections of the deck. Men sleep port side (left) and women on the starboard side (right).

It is supposed to take six days to Manaus. My eye catches "Atlantis" life jackets and a bible verse painted in big black letters on the side of our deck: "John 9:31— We know that God does not hear sinners."

In the bathroom, there are seats on the toilets and a hand basin AND a mirror! All this for a mere R$150 wow! After setting everything up on the deck, we venture off into town to find something to eat, and we decide to support a local 'restaurant' with the name "Bigote do me Tio"—Spanish for

183

A Journey through Many Worlds

"My Uncle's Mustache."

For R$10/kg we buy a type of beef olive with some carrot and bacon in the middle, as well as chicken, fish, rice, beans and some salad. What a feast!

As we finish, I spot a piece of black hair on the side of the plate, and I cannot help thinking about the possible origin of the name " Bigote do me Tio"...

It seems like the whole town is aware of our arrival and although our reception is cold in many cases, some people are very friendly. At one of the local shops, we buy a bottle of Cinzano Bianco and set off back to the boat to enjoy a good rest with a nice sundowner.

+ + + + + +

October 26th, 2002 (Saturday) to 27th 2002 (Sunday)

We take it easy and sort out basics like charging the battery (not so successful because of the cloudy skies and some rain). We also wash our clothing again and buy a few 'Antarctica' beers.

+ + + + + +

October 28th, 2002 (Monday)

Now they say we are leaving at 18h00. There must be about 40 passengers on board now, and they are busy loading cargo—it's hot, and I want to get going!

Chapter 15
On the Amazon heading for Manaus

"I can't say I was ever lost, but I was bewildered once for three days."

—Daniel Boone

It takes eight days to travel and reach Manaus. The vibrant free port city of Manaus is rich in history and has a lively spirit. Today (2002) nearly 1.5 million people are living in Manaus. The city was founded in 1693 as the Fort of São José do Rio Negro. The city is approximately 1500 kilometers from the Atlantic Ocean, and in the 1800's it was called the "Tropical Paris" because of the many wealthy Europeans who settled here during the rubber boom. With them, they brought culture, arts, and music.

The "Teatro Amazonas" (Amazon Theater) was designed by the Italian architect, Celestial Sacardim and was completed in 1896. This magnificent structure deep in the rainforest can seat more than 700 people and was built in Renaissance Revival style from material shipped from Italy, France, Scotland and other countries.

About 10 kilometers from Manaus, the lighter colored Solimões River, rich in Andean sediment, meets the darker water, rich in decayed leaf and plant matter, of the Rio Negro. Because of the different temperature, speed, and density of the two water masses, they flow next to each other for about six kilometers before mixing and becoming part of the lower Amazon river.

We spend a few days in the city of Manaus and then move on by boat to Porto Velho. This city is an important part in the agricultural field because of the soy and other products

185

A Journey through Many Worlds

which are shipped from here down the Rio Madeira, to be transferred onto ocean liners.

+ + + + + +

We sleep over at Porto Velho, and it is here that I receive very sad news from South Africa via Yahoo Chat.

My Mother has passed away.

+ + + + + +

I take a long walk and try to empty my head of thoughts. It is really painful to think that this Lady is gone. Life can be so good. Life can be so terrible.

There is no way that I will be able to reach South Africa very soon, and I must make peace with reality.

+ + + + + +

From Porto Velho to Cuiaba we spend about 20 hours on a bus. From Cuiaba to Saul Paulo it takes another 20 hours, and we book into a clean hotel to refresh, and we will spend two days before catching our flight back as originally planned.

I think about Life.

Why do we make things so complicated? We are alive now. Soon we will be dead. We have a lot of control over most things that happen inbetween life and death. Use it please and LIVE!

186

Chapter 16
The End?

"To travel is to return to strangers."

—Dennis Scott

As we board the Variq flight from Sau Paulo to Johannesburg, I am not looking forward to returning to the world I knew. Mainly because I am aware this world changed a lot. This journey has come to an end, and I guess I must face reality. My dear Mother passed away while I was not at home. I remember well when I saw her last; it was not easy to say goodbye. It was as if I knew it would probably be the last time I will see her. But I had to go.

I am tired both physically and mentally. In the last six months, I learned so much—about the New World we explored, about its people, nature, and wildlife, but also about myself and life. My perception of life. I think back at the Indian incident. It could have turned out so bad, and now I am returning to "normal life"?

I don't honestly see this rat race as "normal," there must be more to life. I miss the river-world.

I spend a few days back at my rented house where my now ex-girlfriend is packing up her belongings to move into another flat in town. For me it's good. It's a new beginning. Sometimes you can trap yourself in a situation where you just continue because it's the easiest way. I promise myself not to do this ever again. Don't get into a relationship if you know deep down inside it will anyway never work. There are much better and cheaper ways to waste time.

I don't want to stay here anymore. This is a chapter that is

A Journey through Many Worlds

closed, and I think I should find a new place.

After spending lots of time in the wild during our six months away, I am looking for a quiet and peaceful place. I am getting really tired of "Hey Johan, we saw what happened to you guys in the Amazon! Tell us the story!!!" And my version became shorter and shorter.

In the local newspaper, the Paarl Post, my eye catches an ad for a "single working person wanted to share house in Paarl."

Not long after that, I move to a smaller house which I share with two friends—Christiaan and Olivia. Christiaan is an energetic gentleman who is in the building and property renovation trade. Olivia is a young lady who is in the catering business, and they welcome me as the new tenant with a glass of wine.

After the unbelievable Andes to Amazon Adventure, I decided that this story needs to be told. I start writing the story from the notes I made during the trip. The six months away from home cost me more than I thought, and as my small bank account quickly diminished in size, I was struggling to get my photography business going again.

If there only was a way to get a decent income to finance my new book venture and to get going with my photography again.

Apparently, there is a lot of new development in the digital photography industry and who knows, maybe in the not too distant future, digital will even replace film! I guess time will tell.

Book II: Return to Riverland

Chapter 1
Back to Reality and Off Again!

"Reality is merely an illusion, albeit a very persistent one."

—Albert Einstein

The Invasion of Iraq by the Coalition Forces which started in March 2003 came to an end in May 2003. This was what America called "Operation Iraqi Freedom." Saddam Hussein was still evading the Coalition Forces in his own country, and the US coalition forces started using subcontractors from different countries through private security companies like Erinys International.

In August 2003, a one year contract of 39.5 million US$ was awarded to Erinys Iraq. Erinys was contracted to recruit, train and implement an Oil Protection Force of 6 500 strong under Task Force Shield, for the protection of about 140 oil sites across Iraq. In Greek mythology, the name "Erinys" originates from the Erinyes (Furies) who were the goddesses of vengeance and retribution who punished the bad guys and guarded the underworld. Through one of my contacts, I get a contact number of somebody involved with recruitment for Erinys, and I thought to give it a try.

I am not new to the world of conflict although I have not been in this trade for quite a while. As I speak over the phone to the lady in charge of recruitment, I get the impression that I can send my CV in but chances of getting appointed are close to zero. There are hundreds, if not thousands of CVs already submitted. But I get her attention when I told her I would email it right away and she can ask Neels, Hennie, and Jakkie who were already employed by Erinys, for references.

Back to Reality and Off Again!

A few days later I receive a phone call telling me to be at Johannesburg Airport in three days to collect my ticket for a flight to Amman, Jordan, where I will meet up with a contact and get further instructions.

To be honest, I didn't expect any reaction after the lady told me of the multitude of applicants. This was great news, but on the other hand, I knew I was a bit 'rusted' and needed to get a quick retraining session before I leave.

I grew up accustomed to weapons and from a young age I used to do target shooting. But I was also taught not to kill just for the sake of killing. Respect life and unless your life is endangered (or you are very hungry of course) thou shall not kill.

I was only 18 when I joined the South African Defence Force. I volunteered for Infantry and was trained as part of a mechanized infantry unit. During what was later known as the "Battle of Cuito Cuanavale," I did active service in Angola, proudly as part of Bravo Company of 61 Mechanised Battalion.

After my two years of service in the South African Army, I became a member of the Cape Town Highlanders; a Citizen Force mechanized infantry regiment. After my military service, I did several jobs and interesting things of which I may tell you another time and maybe in another book.

Then on one beautiful day in the early 1990's, I was on lunch at my not-so-exciting job as the manager at a 'Fotofast' photo lab in Paarl, South Africa. As I paged through one of my favorite magazines called "Soldier of Fortune," my eye caught the trigger word "Angola, " and I read further.

It was a private military company, founded by Eeben Barlow and contracted by the Angolan government to help train its forces to counter the growing threat of the anti government forces who didn't want to accept the outcome of the democratic elections of 1992. But let me not start sharing my thoughts on democracy and history. Bottomline is, I saw an opportunity to possibly earn a better income while doing an exciting job outdoors. And of course, with jobs like this,

A Journey through Many Worlds

one gets to meet interesting people.

I made a few phone calls, sent off my CV with references and about two weeks later I was flying to Johannesburg and on my way to Waterkloof, Pretoria to speak to the Executive Outcomes (EO) officials and sign up.

A few days after the interview I was on my way to an ex Cuban Base at Cabo Ledo, about 120 km south of Luanda. I had such an interesting time there and my experience with EO definitely also helped me with several future employment opportunities. In the international private security field, it is a definite plus if you have been employed by Executive Outcomes. But let's get back to the 'present.'

I made a quick call to an old contact and excellent instructor in close protection as well as firearm and edged weapons training, Keith Conroy. A full day's training camp is set up for the day before my flight to Johannesburg.

I was told that I would probably be issued with a Browning 9mm pistol, so I ask Keith specifically to bring a Browning HP single action pistol to practice with because I have not used this weapon before and just want to get the 'feel' of it. Most of my handgun training and experience is with the CZ 75 and some other brands of pistols. It is an action-filled day with lots of running and many rounds of combat shooting with both the Browning HP and my CZ 75 as well as a Colt AR 15 semi-automatic rifle.

Arriving at Johannesburg International Airport,* I meet several other new Erinys recruits. We are a group of seven in total. It is an interesting assortment of people with ages ranging from the early thirties to around fifty I guess.

---

* South Africa's major airport, originally known as Jan Smuts International Airport, after the 1933 to 1948 Prime Minister of the country. It was renamed Johannesburg International Airport in 1994 when the newly-elected ANC government implemented a national policy of not naming airports after politicians. In spite of this, it was again renamed as O. R. Tambo International Airport on 27 October 2006, by the ANC after Oliver Reginald Tambo, a former President of that party, by which it is still known today.

Back to Reality and Off Again!

I don't recognize any of them, but it becomes apparent that this group represents a variety of backgrounds including Military, South African Police, the Scorpions and one person of an unidentified background. I am sure this is going to get interesting.

We fly to Amman, Jordan, and there we are met by other Erinys security contractors waiting for us. We get into the cars, and the men in khaki clothes and sunglasses take us to the Al Karamah border crossing between Jordan and Iraq.

After a delay that felt like several hours, we drive into Iraq. Less than a kilometer into Iraq we come across several large American SUV's parked on the right side of the desert road and facing forward. We stop and are introduced to the team who are going to do our armed escort to the Erinys Headquarters in Baghdad. We are issued with handguns and AK47's and without waisting time, we drive off towards Baghdad.

The total trip from Amman to Baghdad takes more than 10 hours, and we drive through the towns of Ramadi and Fallujah.

+ + + + + +

After working only a little more than a month in Iraq on my first contract in 2003, we are invited over by an NGO across the street.

We arrive after dark with the standard kit like an AK47, handgun, and grab bag. We had something to drink and chatted to the expats across the street.

At some point, the neighbors, soldiers at the neighboring Italian Carabinieri Headquarters, call us over and invite us to their farewell party. The Italians participated in the Iraq War under Operation Ancient Babylon or Operazione Antica Babilonia.

The next day they will be relieved by a new group, and it is a festive mood on the top floor of the three story building. We have worked with the Italians on several projects and also shared intelligence reports as well as some good food

A Journey through Many Worlds

and even better stories. It was a great evening that ended very early the next morning after a few beers, one more and great pasta. After we had woken up early the next morning, we were off to inspect sites in our area of operation. Our American sector manager, Jeff, stayed at the office.

As we left the oil refinery in Nasseriyah about two hours later, I saw an enormous bright yellow flash of an explosion in front of us, and a moment later the flash turns into a black mushroom shaped cloud of smoke. Then a second or two later the rumbling, deafening thunder crack is heard. The next moment we feel the displacement by hot air through the open windows inside the car, and I know this is World News happening. Not in a good sense.

About 30 people are killed and more than 100 injured as the facade of the same building where we had such a great time very early this morning is ripped off in a devastating suicide attack involving two vehicles. Thinking back at that sight makes me shiver.

When I saw the explosion, I knew it was in the same direction as our Headquarters in Nasseriyah and I call Jeff on the Motorola radio.

"Echo, One do you copy"... crackling... then silence

"Echo One, Echo One—do you copy?"

The crackling stops and after an unnerving silence I hear a hoarse but familiar voice. Jeff Waters is alive and online!!

"This is Echo One—Houston; we have a problem... return to base with extreme caution. A suicide attack and base severely damaged. Many casualties and be careful—high risk, all soldiers, and security are in a state of Weapons Free!".

Weapons free is the order that means you can fire at will.

As we cross the Euphrates river, we are driving not too fast. People are running in different directions. Some to get away and others rush to the scene because they have loved ones that may have been injured or killed. Turmoil, Fear, Anger, Sadness, Shock, Paranoia—those and many more emotions visible everywhere. We enter our home-base slowly from

Back to Reality and Off Again!

a side street. Our Nissan Patrol SUV has got Iraqi number plates. This is usually a good thing and the fact that we don't wear a military uniform, makes us blend in a little more with the locals.

But today, in Iraq and this street particularly it may not be the best of tactics. Especially not if you are armed with AK 47's, submachine guns and sidearms. We lower the weapons to decrease visibility, hands still firm on the grips and trigger fingers ready to slide down and fire within a fraction of a second.

Between us and the blown up building, there are several burning vehicles, injured soldiers, human bodies, parts of bodies, smoke, shattered glass and pieces of building rubble. There are Italian soldiers visible in different positions. Some in the proximity of the partly collapsed building.

I focus on one young man who is clutching his rifle grip so intensely that his knuckles are turning white. Paranoid eyes are darting in every direction. It is as if he is holding a lifeline while scanning for the chopper to appear on the horizon. The eyes of a young soldier in shock. I have seen this before.

+ + + + + +

Our building was repaired after the suicide attack, and after staying at the American Airforce base next to the step pyramid in the ancient city of Ur for a while, we moved back to the same house in town.

+ + + + + +

We are training hundreds of Iraqi people, from young men to some older ex-soldiers who worked under Saddam Hussein. Everybody needs to eat, and the country is in a sorry state after the war.

+ + + + + +

After nine months evading the coalition forces, the Iraqi leader, Saddam Hussein, is caught on 13 December 2003 hiding in a hole near his hometown, Tikrit. I will remember this Saturday very well. We are at our home/office when in a moment all hell broke loose. Shots were being fired from

A Journey through Many Worlds

different directions as we grabbed for our AK47's which we always kept close. Moments later our Interpreter, Falah explains what is happening. "Saddam Hussein was captured! My people are very happy."

A majority of the people near our location in Southern Iraq was glad that he was caught and out of pure happiness they started firing shots off into the air.

A really dangerous and stupid exercise which cost the lives of several innocent people that day. What goes up must come down and depending on the angle of the projectile trajectory, the impact may be fatal.

$$+ + + + + +$$

After my first tour in Iraq that lasted 4 months, I was exhausted. It was a hectic time, and I am glad to be on my way to Baghdad, where we will sleep one night at the Shaheen hotel, before driving to Jordan tomorrow.

As we leave Nasseriyah for Baghdad, the Shaheen Hotel is rocked by the explosion of a 250-kilogram bomb hidden inside a minibus painted with ambulance insignia. Amongst those killed was former South African security policeman, Francois Strydom, who was also working for Erinys. If it was a few hours later, I would have been there too...

$$+ + + + + +$$

On arrival at Johannesburg International Airport, I am stopped and questioned by what appears to be an intelligence agent. This incident makes me worried & I decide that for my next leave I would rather go to another interesting place where South Africans can go without a visa. Thats how I ended up in the beautiful town of Dumfries, Scotland, where I was treated by a lovely English lady called Tracy. It is amazing what can be achieved by internet dating.

$$+ + + + + +$$

Once I completed my 1 year contract with Erinys, Iwas happy to return home. For a short while at least...

Chapter 2

Time-warp 2005—Waking up in a different world

Death tugs at my ear and says: "Live! I am coming."

—Oliver Wendell Holmes, Sr

Like every morning, seven days a week, we must depart at 03h00 and drive from our villa in Kuwait City to the Iraqi border at Safwan. There we will collect our AK47's, Glock pistols, loaded magazines, radios and body armor and do protection of the fuel convoys to a rendezvous point a few hundred kilometers inside Iraq. Depending on what happens we will drive between 600 and 700 kilometers on a 'normal' day between Kuwait and Iraq. We are at present only eight expats working here.

Once we cross the border, we meet up with our armed Iraqi protection teams who will assist us in our duties. Sometimes everything goes strangely smooth, and then you get your impossible days when the fuel convoy consists of more than 300 Petrol (Gasoline) tankers, each carrying 18000 liters of highly flammable fuel.

As we drive home South on the MSR (Military Supply Route) Tampa, I think of what an amazing experience my time in Iraq was.

I came here the first time in October 2003 as one of the team members of a company called Erinys. We were subcontracted by the USA Military to do training of the Oil Police and set up an infrastructure for the protection of the oil installations and later the pipelines.

A Journey through Many Worlds

And boy, we had many close calls. I guess sometime your luck will run out...

The next moment I hear a violent "BANG" and my SUV swerves to the side. I look down at Dacha to my right, and I see the shock in his eyes.

In a fraction-of-a-second, I relive several explosive moments in my life, and it flashes in front of my eyes.

+ + + + + +

1987

It is a humid and hot Angolan day—a few days before Christmas. I am walking towards the ten ton South African Samil Military transport truck carrying ammunition and explosives.

Moments later and a few yards away from my newly dug foxhole, I become aware of the eerie sound of the first of several incoming missiles.

I know the sound because I have heard a Russian 122mm multiple rocket launcher, the BM-21, also called the Grad or "Stalin Organ" before.

The first explosion is an uncomfortably close distance to my right front. The next, less than a second later, to my left and further away. The next one is much closer straight in front of me, another one left and closer. It's running closer to me. I pray.

Impact!!! The next rocket explodes right in front of me, so close that the sand I dug out for the foxhole hours earlier is swept down on my head. I know the next will be my end.

Nothing. Deafening silence. Then my ears are ringing. I open my eyes and I slowly lift my head to look out from the foxhole. I see smoke, cut branches, and trees.

I smile broadly. I am alive! I am 19 and a happy boy.

+ + + + + +

Time-warp 2005

1994

With a fast move, the Angolan colonel grabs his Tokarev pistol from the leather holster on his right hip and kills the soldier with a shot through the head.

The soldier drops in slow motion to the ground, and I hear my ears ringing... Awkward moment and then deafening silence.

+ + + + + +

2007

It's early morning in Kabul, Afghanistan. As I enter the bathroom, I feel the displacement of air and hear, the now familiar sound of an explosion. BABOOM!!! An explosion probably of the suicidal kind. Somebody just blew himself (or herself?) to pieces not far from my work and home. In the name of somebody's religion, many other lives are sacrificed unwillingly.

As I enter the shower moments later, I wonder what we are getting for breakfast this morning.

It is interesting how exposure to situations can change, or "condition" you. I don't see it as insensitive, but rather as well adapted to my situation.

I was taught as part of infantry training that I WILL be able to operate under any conditions and anywhere on this planet. Therefore, I can.

+ + + + + +

What the hell is happening??

I am now looking at myself lying on a hospital trolley. I don't know where this is...I don't really care. Strange feeling. There is some light but not much. There are also people or what appears to be people but I can't really see detail. The only detail I can see is myself. I'm looking at myself from an elevated point somewhere over the right shoulder of my

A Journey through Many Worlds

body. I am not in a panic; I am just observing my body. It feels the natural thing to do.

It goes black. Peaceful...quiet...

"We" are now moving down some steps. Lower and lower as if we are descending into the earth down what looks like ancient stone steps and surrounded by stone walls and ceiling. The little visible light is getting dimmer.

Strangely I don't feel the bumping or anything else as a matter of fact. After all, I am watching myself from a different position—as if the position from where I am observing myself is kind of constant in relation to my body. I don't question what is happening—I am only observing.

It is black again and pain, time, emotion and worries don't exist.

The next moment, or rather the "scene" I observe, is looking at the sun setting in the east. I am on top of what appears to be a step-pyramid (Similar to the Ziggurat at Ur in Iraq) This is real.

There is nobody else, and the only sounds I hear is the Muslim sunset prayer. It is as if I am watching and playing in a movie or rather a reality show. But again there are no real emotions or feeling of pain or fear. This is just how it is. Black again. Nothing.

Johan Dempers is dead.

+ + + + + +

Resuscitation starts immediately in the ambulance and continues as I am brought into ICU. Twelve of my ribs are fractured and one lung damaged.

There are also multiple fractures and abrasions of the chest, back, right shoulder, right thigh, both hands and a broken clavicle. The open wound at the point of impact on my head is bleeding badly.

An emergency open thoracotomy—a cut into the chest wall—has to be performed. The surgeons move fast to gain access to the lungs. The survival rate of resuscitative

200

Time-warp 2005

thoracotomy is only between nine and twelve percent.

A large incision is made on my back, and the ribs are spread apart by retractors. The lung that is damaged is deflated, and chest tubes are inserted between the inner and outer lining of the chest cavity to help drain the bleeding from the pleural space around the lungs.

Abdominal ultrasound reveals severe internal bleeding and another tear is found in the diaphragm.

I start to develop abnormally low blood pressure in spite of fluid replacement, and the decision is made to do a laparotomy. As the surgeons open my chest, it reveals that there is uncontrollable internal bleeding from a splenic tear and a decision is made to remove the spleen immediately.

Aggressive resuscitation is what is saving my life, and I will only find out much later how some of my team members and other staff at Lloyd Owen International (LOI) with "O" blood types kept me alive after I already lost several liters of blood. There is fluid collection within the brain tissue as a result of the trauma caused by impact during the crash.

They put me in a very deep state of unconsciousness by a medically induced coma. This helps to lower the pressure created by the intracranial swelling (brain swelling).

Eighteen days later my condition stabilizes, and I am transferred from ICU to another ward on 28 December 2005. I survived.

+ + + + + +

As I wake up, I get the shock of my life. It is light in my room—I must have overslept! I am confused about what is happening here because I am suddenly aware that there are several people in my room and they are looking at me with different expressions that vary between shock and relief.

As my eyes sweep across the faces, I recognize only one person—Seba. He is the only French person on my team, and he is staring at me with a frown on his face. Now I become aware that we are definitely not in my room on the top floor of our Villa in Kuwait City. As a matter of fact, I don't have any

A Journey through Many Worlds

idea where I am and who these apparently Middle Eastern people are. Shock and Confusion.

I can't move my body!!!!

Am I dreaming?—Is this a nightmare and I will wake up??

"Seba??? Where are we? What is happening?"

Seba's frown deepens.

"JJ, Can't you remember the accident???" Seba asks in his unique smoky voice and French accent.

I am called by my initials because they struggle to say "Johannes Jurgens" in the way it should be said.

As I look down, I become aware that my bare chest is riddled with scars from stitches running down my chest to my abdomen. What is more shocking is that they appear to be old scars that have healed or partially healed already!...

SEBA????

Everything is black again. No Sound. No Pain. No Feeling. Nothing...

+ + + + + +

What happened was that we were returning home after doing convoy security in Iraq. I was driving down the three-lane, French built MSR Highway towards Kuwait City in a black GMC Envoy SUV.

Dacha, my Bosnian team member, was strapped in next to me and he was relaxing in his seat, partially lowered, after a long days work.

According to the GPS found afterward at the crash site, we were traveling at about 170 km/hour when something caused a blowout of a rear tire. The SUV violently swerved first left into a barrier next to the road and then bounced back to the right and in front of a twenty-ton tanker speeding down the right lane. The extreme force of impact of the tankers bull-bar on the left rear of the SUV left it totally out of control as it hit an embankment just off the side of the road. The right front wheel and the rim were completely ripped off as the

202

Time-warp 2005

SUV's front was smashed out of proportion.

The colossal crash into the embankment caused my body to be forcibly ejected through the side window, and the impact of my body against the metal caused the instant fracturing of several bones, and my left shoulder humeral head was crushed.

My body was flung from the car and crashed onto the rocky desert landscape about 20 meters (65 feet) from the car wreck with Dacha still strapped inside.

Only moments after the crash another SUV stops on the scene. What his name was and who he worked for I will never know, but this young Muslim man knew the basics of " the first responder."

He did an assessment and checked my airways first and saved my life by calling the emergency services for assistance. Shortly after that, the ambulances, police and traffic police were on the scene, and Daca and myself were lifted and rushed to the Al Jahra Hospital which was the closest intensive care unit (ICU) to us.

+ + + + + +

My progression is slow, and it takes some time to get the drugs out of your system. I sleep a lot every day, and when awake, I don't feel exceptionally good.

Some days I wake up and get flashbacks of past moments of trauma and action in my life. Some days I remember my name and other days I don't know who I am and I don't recognize anybody. I cannot concentrate and to read a full sentence is really too much. I get a lot of support from my team members as well as the office people who come and visit regularly. Sometimes I am in good spirits, and the next moment I feel as if I am under attack again. Slowly but surely I regain my perception of the 'here and now'—life must go on.

As I am starting to regain memory, I also feel more irritated and frustrated. When I leave the hospital to return to my company headquarters, a Phillipino lady is appointed

203

A Journey through Many Worlds

to be my assistant and nurse. I have been on nasogastric tube feeding and artificial hydration for weeks and could not normally eat at all for a total of about two months now.

Now I find it difficult to eat again, and my weight is at present only around 45 kilograms. I lost nearly 30kg of weight—before the crash, I weighed 74kg.

A few months ago I was the biggest carnivore imaginable. Meat and especially red meat is my food of choice in normal life, but when my other Bosnian friend and team mate, Elvir Delilac, walks into the room with a nice juicy Kuwaiti beef burger that he especially bought for me, I have an immediate and adverse reaction.

I don't like the smell of meat at this moment, and I am craving for fresh tomato and lettuce. Is this a spontaneous reaction of the body because it is telling me what it needs right now? Is my body telling me to say "No!" to meat because my digestive system knows it will have a terrible time coping with a sudden load of solid meat? This is really weird. What I find interesting is that the thought of eating meat is suddenly not a good thought. My body is slowly adapting to retaking solid foods.

Next to my bed is my wheelchair. Since I regained my consciousness, I am in a lot of pain, and my right leg doesn't have any feeling. From the thigh down it feels like an artificial limb. My room is on the lower level of the building, and after about a week I request that the nurse move to another room and I will call her when I need help. The pain pills keep me asleep several hours a day.

I wake up early one morning, just after midnight, worried and thinking of my parents. I haven't spoken to them since the crash, and I am especially worried about my mother.

I know she is recovering from a stroke and I know the news about my accident will have a very negative impact on her health. I also realize that my current mental state is affecting my speech to such a degree that speaking to them will not be a good idea. About two days later I wake up, and it is as if a time curtain lifts. I remember with a shock that my mother

204

Time-warp 2005

passed away in November 2002...more than three years ago while I was on a photographic expedition in the Amazon! I remember receiving the terrible news via the internet when we reached one of the bigger towns in the rainforest.

I am terribly tired and to be honest I feel like I am dying. It doesn't really worry me—it is just the way I am feeling.

+ + + + + +

My convoy protection team members visit me regularly. I am delighted to find out Dacha is fine and he had much fewer injuries than me.

Alan Waller, CEO of the company employing me, also visits. He tells me that they have filed a medical claim and that they are doing everything possible to assist me. I am very grateful but frustrated because no doctor is visiting me and nobody is giving me any proper feedback regarding my medical condition.

Will I be able to walk again? If so, when? What caused the accident? Was it investigated properly? I hear all kind of rumors about a possible attack, sabotage of the vehicle, and more. I cannot remember anything.

At this stage, I don't really care, and I only feel like going home. South Africa. I want to see the blue skies again and feel the African sun on my skin. I miss my country, and I want to be there.

I am tired of being in pain and hospitals. Right now I don't care if I can walk or not. I just want to be in my world surrounded by things I know and love. Smell nature, to see green vineyards, and mountains, white clouds against the deep blue African sky.

+ + + + + +

Alan Waller arranges a flight home for me. I only have good things to say about Emirates Airlines and their assistance is excellent. I am helped into a specially adapted airline wheelchair and then lifted in a wheelchair elevator next to the plane and allowed to enter at the special side entrance for business class. I didn't tell anybody back home exactly

A Journey through Many Worlds

when I am returning, and this is a very tiring trip flying from Kuwait City to Dubai, then Johannesburg and Cape Town.

About ten minutes before landing I am looking down at the beautiful, welcoming landscape of the Winelands area called Boland. After landing in Cape Town, I am assisted with the collection of my luggage, and I end up sitting at a table in a restaurant in Cape Town International Airport.

I am ravenous, and I haven't had anything to eat since leaving Kuwait City. I was too scared to eat because I did not know how I would be able to get to and use the onboard toilet. But before I eat, I need to arrange transport back to Wellington.

+ + + + + +

Before I departed Kuwait, I asked an old friend to book accommodation for me at a guesthouse that's wheelchair friendly in Wellington, my old hometown. Usually, when I come home for my R&R (Military slang for Rest and Recreation), I will go to Somerset West, but because the flat I am renting is on the first floor and there are only stairs, it will not be a smart decision for right now.

I phone Johan Fourie who was also doing security work in Iraq before and ask him if he can arrange transport for me to Wellington. Johan says he will make a plan and I know he will.

I can't remember the last time I was this hungry, so I order myself a kiddies breakfast, but I cannot finish all the chips. My stomach cannot handle all this so fast.

Not long after, Fourie enters the restaurant. I see him looking from left to right, trying to find me. His eyes sweep past me, then freezes a moment and turns back slowly. As he focuses on me, his eyes widen to a disproportionate size, and he utters the words "FUCKING HELL" slightly too loud for normal restaurant standards.

He walks up to me sitting in my wheelchair with a fixed gaze, and I get the impression that I must be looking worse than I thought. Fourie sits down, and we start chatting.

206

Time-warp 2005

He tells me about some of the rumors that went around, including one that my vehicle was hit by an IED (Improvised explosive device) attack.

Earlier this year my regular team mate, Llubisa Aleksic, got killed in an IED attack while on a mission near Baghdad. I would have been in the vehicle, but I was sent on leave just before the trip. Elvir (Tyson) Delilac was with Llubisa and narrowly escaped death. In this incident and the mayhem that followed, we had a few members killed and two missing in action. A shit time and I had to return early from leave.

At one point it was only myself and Seba, my French connection, that manned the big convoys as international security team members. Some days I had to work alone when Seba had another priority. Luckily we were assisted by Iraqi security, and we trusted them with our lives. They were great people that never betrayed us.

While Fourie drives me back to Wellington, I think about how fast things can change in your life. Not only in war zones, but also in "normal life." Live to the full as if there is no tomorrow because one day it will be true and there will be no tomorrow.

Will I walk again? I have no feeling in my right leg. I visit Dr. Patrick Fieuw, and he refers me to a neurosurgeon. In short, he says there is permanent upper motor neuron damage, and it's not possible to know for sure that I will be able to walk again.

I see several doctors and spend a few weeks at a sub-acute medical facility in Paarl for rehabilitation. While here an old friend comes to visit. I have known Hugo for many years, and he is in the planning and construction industry. His daughter, Muldene, also visits and she tells me about the photography and graphic design course she is busy with in Stellenbosch. The girl I saw three years ago has turned into a lovely lady.

++++++

Unfortunately, because of the medical and accommodation costs, my funds are now disappearing fast, and I take up

207

A Journey through Many Worlds

a very kind offer from my friend Arthur to visit and stay with him and his family in Johannesburg. Apparently, there is a facility doing hydro-therapy which they highly recommended.

So off I go to Johannesburg, and Arthur is standing, waiting for me as I roll my wheelchair into the arrivals hall at Johannesburg International Airport.

It was hard work, and I will be forever grateful to Arthur for inviting me and taking me to the physiotherapist three times each week to receive hydrotherapy. I also received occupational therapy sessions.

Through dedication, support and the will to win, I can now rise from the wheelchair and give my first unsupported step in more than six months. As I return to Wellington a few months later, I can leave my wheelchair behind in Johannesburg.

In the meantime, Alan Waller is still making promises via email that he is "fighting my case" with the insurance company and that I must keep all my bills, etc. I will get reimbursed he promises.

The original company I was working for, Lloyd Owen International, has now closed down and I am starting to realize that the "insurance" issue might be more a case of, "There is no insurance."

I asked several times for details about the policy and reports of the accident/incident I was involved in but only get vague answers and a few copies of documents that were apparently sent off by Alan or his secretary.

Time for action.

Chapter 3
Against all Odds—
Mission Afghanistan and Back to Jordan and Iraq

Alan Waller is now in Jordan and apparently busy with a new "project." I take my accumulated Skyward miles from my previous Emirates Flights between South Africa and Iraq and book a return ticket to Amman, Jordan. Only after making the booking, I email Alan and tell him I am on my way. His answer follows shortly after my email, and he tells me I am very welcome to visit, but he has a job offer for me in Afghanistan if I should be interested.

Well, to be very honest, that decision was instant, and within a few days, I was off again on a flight to Kabul, Afghanistan via Dubai. It was a matter of "money talks," and I was very broke after paying all my medical fees while not working.

I spent a total of seven months in Afghanistan on a contract, and I am employed as an operations officer for International Medical and Rescue. Our task was to deliver medical assistance to our members which included the United Nations and several high profile clients and security companies. We had medical doctors, nurses, as well as an air wing with helicopters and fixed wing planes at our disposal to do emergency evacuations and repatriations from anywhere within our area of operation to any destination around the globe.

It was mostly an exciting time, and I took the opportunity to rent the only single prop aircraft in the whole of Afghanistan. The reason why there is only one single prop airplane here is apparent. In this unfriendly and uneven

A Journey through Many Worlds

terrain, one would prefer to have any backup possible. This is also true when it comes to air transport and propellers. The small Cessna 210 with the little sticker next to the door that indicates that no assault weapons are allowed onboard, belongs to a humanitarian organization called Pactec and the pilot today is Iwan Hess.

The temperature on the ground is minus 25 degrees Celsius as we await the departure of the gigantic Russian IL76 military transport aircraft. This monster has a maximum take off weight of 190 tons. I would like to capture some images of the Bamyan area where the Taliban destroyed the 1700-year-old Budha statues in the Hindu Kush mountains early in 2001 in a stupid act of power.

Long ago the trade between the Middle East and China used to pass through Bamyan, and it was part of the Silk Route of many, many moons ago.

As we fly past the huge openings in the mountain, where the gigantic statues stood not so long ago, I capture some images on camera. It's sad that I cannot see the original work and I think again about the power of photography. A camera gives you the magical ability to capture Time. The landscape and people I photograph now will never look the same again. Time change faces as well as landscapes. Time changes everything to a certain extent.

With the wind chill factor taken into account, the temperature at the open window is now close to 50 degrees below freezing point, and my hands are in pain. I am worried that the battery on my Canon 1DsMk2 camera will not last long and I put the backup battery tighter between my legs to try and retain temperature. After landing later at the 2200 meter (2 562 ft) lonely asphalt runway, we are met by a few locals, and I use the opportunity to take some photos.

I spent a total of seven months and logged 17 suicide attacks in Kabul and surrounds. Our highly capable medical team including doctors, nurses and paramedics saved many lives and made a big difference to many people and families around the world.

Against all Odds

But now it was time to move on. For my leave, I book a flight, not back home to South Africa, but to Amman, Jordan. Alan Waller, my super evasive employer was here somewhere, and I would like to sit down and chat with him about the insurance claim he allegedly was handling after the Kuwait car accident which cost me a large part of my mobility and very nearly my whole life.

I can't get hold of Waller in Amman and book into a great hotel that Dr. Munther Zureigat, who worked with me in Afghanistan, recommended.

While I am here, I might as well do some excellent photography. I take a bus down to the coastal city of Aqaba, on the southern most point of Jordan. Here I charter a plane and am lucky enough to have the beautiful Miss Basmah Bani (Later she became a Princess of Jordan) as the pilot. She was Jordan's first female pilot to obtain an aerobatics certificate.

We do two flights, one around the world famous "Rose City" of Petra and one over the Magical sandstone and granite landscape of Wadi Rum, also known as "The Valley of the Moon." Beautiful days with beautiful weather.

I am lucky enough to find a good bottle of Cabernet Sauvignon from one of the top Stellenbosch wine farms which I give to Basmah as a token of appreciation for her fantastic company and professionalism.

As I book out of the Golden Tulip hotel, I ask my taxi driver if he can take me to Wadi Rum. I love semi-desert landscapes, and I spend about a week here living alone in a bedouin tent, shooting sunsets, drinking camel milk and trying to communicate with stones. It is amazing how a landscape can transform my mood, and I am feeling well rested when I call my taxi driver again to pick me up and take me to an incredible city carved out of stone. The city of Petra. I remember seeing Petra as the backdrop in a scene from the Indiana Jones movie, "Raiders of the Lost Ark."

I will never forget Petra and all the historical treasures of Jordan. There are so many untold stories of this great

A Journey through Many Worlds

Kingdom.

My next move is to Kurdistan, Northern Iraq, where I am part of a small team tasked to set up a medical support base for groups of expats working north of Dohuk, towards the Turkish border. Paramedic Lyle Simes and Doctor Munther Zureigat also joins us.

Here I spent most of my time working from the top story of the Dilshad Palace Hotel, monitoring the security of the seismic operations and coordinating communications between my headquarters in Amman and the field team in Dohuk.

Again I have the honor to meet good people. Ayad Brifkani is our driver here, but Ayad is much more than a driver. He is an honorable young man, a qualified teacher and a highly talented sculpture.

As my year contract is closing there is yet again problems with our evasive employer and Ayad is also not getting his salary as promised. I give him some extra money simply because I can see what he is doing and I really respect him.

When I see my salary is yet again not transferred into my account as promised, I send a message to Waller that I am going home. I have heard enough promises and the money he owes me, I will never see. The paramedic, Lyle Simes, is also resigning, and this adventure is over —it's time for a change.

Ayad drives me to the Erbil Airport and greets me with tears in his eyes. "Take care my Brother JJ." I miss Ayad and wish I can revisit one day again.

It's August 2008, And I arrive back in Cape Town, just a few days before Muldene finishes her photography contract for Carnival Cruise Lines in the Caribbean.

A new chapter starts.

Chapter 4
Some Thoughts

When Joe Brooks visited the Amazon nearly 55 years ago, he met somebody called Bob Webb. I also mentioned Bob in the first section of the book. Bob is an interesting man, a real adventurer and also later in life a motivational speaker.

I spoke to Bob, now in his 80's, at the beginning of this year (2017), and he said I can share the following wise words with you:

1. Set a goal and follow a path.

The path has mini goals that go in many directions. When you learn to succeed at mini goals, you will be motivated to challenge grand goals.

2. Finish what you start.

A half finished project is of no use to anyone. Quitting is a habit. Develop the habit of finishing self-motivated projects.

3. Socialize with others of similar interest.

Mutual support is motivating. We will develop the attitudes of our five best friends. If they are losers, we will be a loser. If they are winners, we will be a winner. To be a cowboy we must associate with cowboys.

A Journey through Many Worlds

4. Learn how to learn.

Dependency on others for knowledge supports the habit of procrastination. Man has the ability to learn without instructors. In fact, when we learn the art of self-education we will find, if not create, opportunity to find success beyond our wildest dreams.

5. Harmonize natural talent with interest that motivates.

Natural talent creates motivation, motivation creates persistence and persistence gets the job done.

6. Increase knowledge of subjects that inspires.

The more we know about a subject, the more we want to learn about it. A self-propelled upward spiral develops.

7. Take risk.

Failure and bouncing back are elements of motivation. Failure is a learning tool. No one has ever succeeded at anything worthwhile without a string of failures.

Chapter 5
15 Years Later —
A New Adventure Unfolds

Wow! It's 2017 and 15 Years since we departed on our crazy adventure to the Andes and Amazon in 2002. Muldene and I have been together for more than a decade and I am still the luckiest guy in the world to have such a partner. Muldene asked a few times before why we can't do another expedition to the Amazon. Well... maybe I didn't think she was serious.

Sometime last year I tested a new software photo collage program and printed a collage of our old Andes to Amazon pictures.

This poster I put up in my studio, and after a few months, I suddenly realized that in 2017 it would be 15 years ago! Well, why not! We can do another expedition if we want. But let's combine education with it I think.

I remember that after the previous trip I was contacted by a school in the United States and the teacher told me that they would really love to be part of any future expeditions. "Not in a physical way, but maybe we can send you requests, or you can record stuff for us while you are there. It will be great if the children can feel they are part of the adventure!"

On a Sunday around November 2016, I asked Muldene if she would really like to do an expedition to the Amazon. "OF COURSE!!!", she replied. This redhead girl is not your average girl. I took my phone and called Joe Brooks.

"Yes, I would love to if it's possible", is Joe's reply. So we have three people now. I suggest we take another person with to complete two teams of two.

215

A Journey through Many Worlds

My first thought is Hennie van Rooyen. I have known Hennie for many years and he is a dedicated, loyal, honest and reliable man. My first choice for another team member. I call Hennie and a few minutes later, we have our team for the next adventure! My trusty 26 year old green Karrimor Jaguar 8 backpack that saw action in Angola, Mozambique, Iraq, Aghanistan, Dubai, Kurdistan, Jordan, Peru and Brazil will once again be securing my kit.

Now, this is exactly what we intend to do: We will be flying out of Cape Town on 16 August 2017 via Luanda, Angola to Sao Paulo, Brazil.

There we will meet with the same Federal Police agent that debriefed us after our incident with the Indians 15 years ago.

From Sao Paulo, we are going to Acre province where we plan to meet up with researchers who found fascinating evidence of past civilization in the jungle.

But that will only be the beginning of an amazing new adventure with lots of exciting things to be learned and shared.

Please follow us and be part of this Adventure in another world.

Johan Dempers,

Expedition Amazon 2017

'No man ever steps in the same river twice, for it's not the same river, and he is not the same man.'

—*Heraclitus*

My final message in this book must be:
Always be honest with yourself and work in the direction of bettering yourself and the world around you. Appreciate and use any opportunities that you are offered and remember that this too shall come to an end. Live for the moment, but always keep the future in mind.

> *'My friend, always remember this: Life consists of Moments...Chapters - same as a book. Make the most of the chapter you are in because it will come to an end. Sometimes very fast. And eventually, the book will end too.'*
>
> — *A Sniper I once knew*

- THE BEGINNING -

Lightning Source UK Ltd.
Milton Keynes UK
UKHW012307070223
416610UK00001B/94